Essays and Studies 1992

The English Association

The object of the English Association is to promote the knowledge and appreciation of English language and literature.

The Association pursues these aims by creating opportunities of co-operation among all those interested in English; by furthering the recognition of English as essential in education; by discussing methods of English teaching; by holding lectures, conferences, and other meetings; by publishing a journal, books, and leaflets; and by forming local branches overseas and at home.

Publications

The Year's Work in English Studies. An annual bibliography. Published by Blackwell (U.S.A.: Humanities Press).

Essays and Studies. An annual volume of essays by various scholars assembled by the collector covering usually a wide range of subjects and authors from the medieval to the modern. Published by D.S. Brewer.

English. The journal of the Association, *English* is published three times a year by the Association.

Newsletter. A *Newsletter* is published three times a year giving information about forthcoming publications, conferences, and other matters of interest.

Benefits of Membership

Institutional Membership

Full members receive copies of *The Year's Work in English Studies*, *Essays and Studies*, *English* (3 issues) and three *Newsletters*.

Ordinary Membership covers *English* (3 issues) and three *Newsletters*.

Schools Membership includes two copies of each issue of *English*, one copy of *Essays and Studies*, three *Newsletters*, and preferential booking and rates for various conferences held by the Association.

Individual Membership

Individuals take out Basic Membership, which entitles them to buy all regular publications of the English Association at a discounted price, and attend Association gatherings.

For further details write to The Secretary, The English Association, The Vicarage, Priory Gardens, London W4 1TT.

Essays and Studies 1992

Percy Bysshe Shelley
Bicentenary Essays

Edited by
Kelvin Everest

for the English Association

D. S. BREWER

ESSAYS AND STUDIES 1992
IS VOLUME FORTY-FIVE IN THE NEW SERIES
OF ESSAYS AND STUDIES COLLECTED ON BEHALF OF
THE ENGLISH ASSOCIATION
ISSN 0071-1357

First published 1992 by D. S. Brewer, Cambridge

D. S. Brewer is an imprint of Boydell & Brewer Ltd
PO Box 9, Woodbridge, Suffolk IP12 3DF, UK
and of Boydell & Brewer Inc.
PO Box 41026, Rochester, NY 14604, USA

ISBN   0 85991 352 X

British Library Cataloguing-in-Publication Data
Percy Bysshe Shelley : Bicentenary Essays. –
(Essays & Studies Series, ISSN 0071-1357;
Vol. 45)
I. Everest, Kelvin II. Series
821.7
ISBN 0-85991-352-X

The Library of Congress has cataloged this serial publication:
Catalog card number 36-8431

The paper used in this publication meets the minimum requirements
of American National Standard for Information Sciences –
Permanence of Paper for Printed Library Materials, ANSI Z39.48-1984

Printed in Great Britain by
St Edmundsbury Press Ltd, Bury St Edmunds, Suffolk

Contents

Preface

There has been a recovery in Shelley's reputation since the end of the second world war. It has been effected by the work mainly of American and British critics and scholars, and has managed a noticeable acceleration over the past two decades, the twenty years or so leading up to the bicentenary of the poet's birth in 1992. The attacks of Eliot and Leavis, and the generally anti-Romantic cast of Modernist thinking and critical practice, had reduced Shelley's stature on the grounds of a slack and self-regarding critical intelligence. He was regarded by many influential voices in the literary academy as given to woolly and even morally dubious idealism in ethics and politics. These qualities of mind were further seen as inextricably bound up with corresponding weaknesses of poetic style. There is no longer any need to rehearse the critical characterisations in any substance; they are familiar enough, and easily recovered in, for example, various still in-print popular or student guides to English Literature.

The grounds of the recovery in critical reputation have not been political, although the grounds of the earlier attacks often were, implicitly or not. It has not been a question of the recovery by a radical culture of the voice and achievements of the most radical thinker in the English literary tradition. Such recoveries have not in fact been necessary; Shelley has always been alive in the culture of the Left in Britain. The work of Paul Foot, for instance, was not revolutionary in its view of Shelley as a sophisticated, informed, and deeply persuasive and influential writer on the side of the people's struggle. That was the received view within the political culture; *Red Shelley* was more concerned to reaffirm these qualities in Shelley's achievement for a new generation, educated by a literary-academic establishment which had lost sight of them.

Neither had the change in Shelley's stature owed anything, at least in any obvious or direct way, to the rise of Feminism in political life generally, even though this rise has been very noticeable and increasingly powerful in the academic study of literature. On the contrary, Shelley's own fully explicit and fully committed feminism has, if anything, proved a problem for his critical reputation amongst feminist critics. The very openness of its articulation has laid bare contradictions and difficulties which have more readily attracted censure, particularly in connection with a perhaps justifiable determination to elevate and establish Mary Shelley as an important writer.

There have however been implicit political interests at work in one area where Shelley has benefited from critical attention over the past twenty years. In some dominant strains of the debate about theory and literary criticism, Shelley has been placed deliberately at the centre of argument. The influential Yale collaboration *Literature and Deconstruction* used Shelley in this way, and critics interested in a view of language drawing on the work of Derrida and De Man have repeatedly turned to Shelley as a writer whose style can be thought of as a continual process of self-undermining rhetorical self-consciousness. With isolated exceptions, this kind of work has been carried out by American academics working in the American system.

A second factor in the revaluation of Shelley has been the tremendous amount of scholarly energy and resources devoted to the textual problem. The problem itself is now quite widely recognised and understood, but its sheer scale and complexity have attracted growing numbers of younger scholars to work on the various diplomatic and conventional scholarly editions of the poetry, prose, letters, and miscellaneous manuscript material which are now under way. This has produced a further effect in the context of broader recent developments in literary research. The whole question of the provenance and status of literary texts has become suddenly central, with the realisation that issues in literary theory take on their sharpest edge when they are brought into relation with problems of editorial practice. Shelley has thus quickly become a 'site' for the exploration of difficult and momentous questions about the authority and determinate substantive forms in which literary texts exist and are transmitted through time.

One essay in the present collection attempts to focus on some of the issues involved in this area. The most important recent textual work on Shelley has been done mainly by Americans, again (although by no means exclusively), and has been carried forward in an American context. There has, though, been a third factor in Shelley's revival. He has attracted a growing number of acutely subtle and sympathetically inward *readers*; that is to say, critics who start from the assumption that Shelley was and most importantly still is to be understood as a skilful practising writer, whose work takes what point it can ever really have only from the quality of his achievements simply as a writer. This approach has found its excellent American practitioners – the work of William Keach in particular springs to mind – but it has been a distinct feature of recent British book-length studies, and it has been partly nourished by a native British tradition of untheorised attention to the precise workings and qualities of Shelley's poetry, considered as a body of work which continues to live within a living literary culture. It is academic in character, but its sense of Shelley is not wholly circumscribed or determined by an academic agenda. Most of the essays in the present collection – all of them by British academics – address themselves to Shelley's distinctive qualities as a writer, and they ground their judgements in the assumption that it is in such terms that Shelley continues to be important; not as a factor in larger debates, about theory or about scholarly practice, or about the place of political belief and commitment in academic life, but as a writer whose primary and fundamental vitality is to be discovered in the way that he writes.

Shelley's 'Dream of Youth':
Alastor, 'Selving' and the Psychic Realm

VINCENT NEWEY

In an essay of 1916 Sigmund Freud tells how he had been walking through a delightful countryside with a young but famous poet, and how the latter had been unable to take any interest in the scene because it seemed to him to be 'shorn of its worth by the transience which was its doom'.[1] Even had the event taken place a hundred years before, the poet could not have been Shelley. For Shelley transience was always a source of fascination and added value. Nowhere is this more apparent than in his first volume of poetry, *Alastor: or, the Spirit of Solitude, and Other Poems*, which was published in 1816:[2] not only does the title poem engage lingeringly with the problem of mortality itself, but the several accompanying pieces take up the theme of transitoriness and change in a variety of registers.

Probably the best-known of these lyrics ponders a falling-away in the particular life of a figure with whom Shelley was currently much preoccupied – Wordsworth, whose new-found conservatism (Shelley had just read, for example, the address to 'the State and Church of England' in *The Excursion* of 1814)[3] prompts a defiant lament for the passing of 'lone star' days:

---

[1] Sigmund Freud, 'On Transience' (1916), *The Pelican Freud Library, Volume 14: Art and Literature*, ed. Albert Dickson (Harmondsworth, 1985), p. 287.
[2] All references to poems from the *Alastor* volume, and to all other poems for the period 1804–1817, are taken from *The Poems of Shelley*, Volume I, ed. Geoffrey Matthews and Kelvin Everest, Longman Annotated English Poets (London and New York, 1989): hereafter *POS*. For poems after 1817, reference is to *Shelley: Poetical Works*, ed. Thomas Hutchinson, corrected G. M. Matthews (2nd edn, Oxford, 1970): hereafter *PW*.
[3] Mary Shelley notes on 14 September 1814: 'Shelley . . . calls on Hookham and brings home Wordsworth's "Excursion" of which we read a part, much disappointed. He is a slave' (*The Journals of Mary Shelley*, ed. Paula R. Feldman and Diana Scott-Kilvert (Oxford, 1987), i. 25). The importance of Shelley's response to Wordsworth in *Alastor* and the associated poems was first explored in detail by Paul Mueschke and Earl L. Griggs in 'Wordsworth as the Prototype of the Poet in Shelley's *Alastor*', *PMLA*, xlix (1934), 229–45. Among the several more recent treatments of the subject, the richest, and the most diffi-

1

> In honoured poverty thy voice did weave
> Songs consecrate to truth and liberty,–
> Deserting these, thou leavest me to grieve,
> Thus having been, that thou shouldst cease to be.
>   ('To Wordsworth', ll. 11–14)

This account of Wordsworth's apostasy has links with the lines on the 'Fall of Bonaparte' which condemn both Napoleon's descent from libertarianism to imperialism and the greater corporate 'Crime' of the Bourbon restoration after Waterloo.[4] Political concerns, however, are less in evidence in the volume than experiential ones – surprisingly perhaps in view of the fact that Shelley's previous major work, *Queen Mab* (1813), had been a systematic attack upon the corruptness of human institutions. 'Stanzas. – April 1814', for instance, which are Shelley's response to his own ill-fated infatuation with Cornelia Boinville Turner, realize an immediate sense of past moments, distilled to images, surviving simultaneously as curse and blessing: in the conclusion that 'deep musings are not free / From the music of two voices and the light of one sweet smile' (ll. 23–24) feelings of confinement blend inextricably with those of pleasure, expressing a characteristic Shelleyan ambivalence. 'Thou in the grave shalt rest', says Shelley in these 'Stanzas'; but in the verses on 'A Summer-Evening Churchyard, Lechlade, Gloucestershire' the grave becomes the site neither of simple repose nor of ending (for 'rest' ambiguously suggests both) but of possible access to a privileged realm of truth and vision, as the poet moves from a delight in the evening scene, with 'dusky braids' and sun-set 'pyramids of fire', to a final hope that death hides 'sweet secrets'. Thus Shelley valorizes the ultimate transformation. Similarly, in 'Mutability' he then embraces brevity and restlessness as the inescapable condition of humankind:

> We are as clouds that veil the midnight moon;
>   How restlessly they speed, and gleam, and quiver,
> Streaking the darkness radiantly! – yet soon
>   Night closes round, and they are lost for ever: (ll. 1–4)

cult, is Yvonne M. Carothers, '*Alastor*: Shelley Corrects Wordsworth', *Modern Language Quarterly*, xlii (1981), 21–47. See also Wasserman, cited in n. 7 below.
[4]   See also the unpublished translation of Guido Cavalcanti's sonnet to Dante, 'Returning from its daily quest, my Spirit': *POS*, pp. 453–54.

There is as much of imaginative excitement as of regret in this, and the poem ends on a note that strains beyond acceptance towards celebration of mutability as perpetual flux – 'Man's yesterday may ne'er be like his morrow; / Nought may endure but Mutability' (ll. 15–16).

Shelley's position resembles that of Freud himself, whose reply to his pessimistic companion is that, though the 'temporal limitation' of things is a painful reality, it does not lessen, and may well increase, their 'significance for our own emotional lives'.[5] The significance of vulnerability and death, and indeed of worldly achievement, for Shelley's emotional life at the time of the *Alastor* volume, however, has a special force, for, as Mary Shelley reports, 'physical suffering had . . . considerable influence in causing him to turn his eyes inward; inclining him rather to brood over the thoughts and emotions of his own soul than to glance abroad . . . In the Spring of 1815 an eminent physician pronounced that he was dying of a consumption'.[6] Earl Wasserman's standard account of *Alastor* presents it as a dialectic between the viewpoints of the Narrator, who is a Wordsworthian figure bound to the finite world of Nature, and the Visionary, or Poet, who pursues an impossible infinite perfection; and so the poem becomes 'one kind of poetry contemplating another', and a crafted expression of Shelley's scepticism.[7] This is helpful, as we shall see, but it obscures the nature of the work as dynamic, and unstable, mental topography revealing Shelley's inner life, urges, confusions, and endeavour to work things out during a period of extraordinary crisis. *Alastor* is, in Christine Gallant's term, 'concentrical' as well as dialectical; it does exist, contrary to Wasserman's assertion, 'in a single range of reference', which is the poet's overarching psyche.[8] The point can be underlined by looking at one more of the shorter poems of 1816.

Mary Shelley records that 'O! there are spirits' 'was addressed in idea to Coleridge',[9] but it is clear that Coleridge becomes, if not quite a double of Shelley, then at least a character through whom he takes the measure of aspects of his own situation and outlook. The first two

---

5 'On Transience', p. 288.
6 Mary Shelley, 'Note on *Alastor*' (1839): *PW*, p. 30.
7 Earl R. Wasserman, *Shelley: A Critical Reading* (Baltimore and London, 1971), pp. 11–41.
8 Christine Gallant, *Shelley's Ambivalence* (London, 1989), p. 21.
9 Mary Shelley, 'Note on the Early Poems' (1839): *POS*, p. 448.

stanzas describe the addressee's naive Romantic faith in active recipro-
city with Nature (Coleridge's theory of the One Life 'within us and
abroad'), and the eventual failure of that philosophy when 'winds',
'springs' and 'moonlight seas' 'Cast, like a worthless boon, thy love
away' (ll. 7–12). Stanza three then talks of another lost union – the
erotic love that must be renounced, for 'Thou hast sought in starry
eyes / Beams that were never meant for thine' (ll. 13–14). This seems
to conflate thoughts of Coleridge's thwarted desire for Sara Hutchinson with Shelley's memories of his own affair with Harriet Grove.[10]
But outward facts are less important than the drama within as Shelley
finds these two centres of inspiration and stability, 'natural scenes' and
'human smiles', both wanting and then in the next lines develops an
apparent answer to their untrustworthiness by an appeal to the idea of
self-sufficiency ('Did thine own mind afford no scope / Of love, or
moving thoughts to thee?'), only to see that way forward compromised
by a realization of the precariousness of the 'soul': 'Thine own soul still
is true to thee, / But changed to a foul fiend through misery' (ll.
29–30). In a well-known passage from the prose fragment 'On Love',
written in 1818, the 'prototype', or beloved, that Shelley proposes to
pursue for fulfilment is a 'miniature as it were of our entire self': 'if we
feel, we would that another's nerves should vibrate to our own, that
the beams of their eyes should kindle at once and mix and melt into
our own'.[11] He was just as forcibly conscious, however, of how easily
the self-generated and self-reflecting image could turn into a 'ghastly
presence' or a 'scourge', as it does in 'O! there are spirits', which ends
with a warning against the 'pangs' that would arise from chasing the
soul-turned-fiend. The biological metaphor by which the Romantics
regularly described poetic process is wholly appropriate to a poem like
'O! there are spirits'. The text is an outgrowth of the mind. It at once
discusses and enacts psychological quest, and brings into focus both
the search for plenitude and the dark underside which is vacancy,
introversion or despair.[12] So, on a much larger scale, does *Alastor*.

In a fine essay on *Alastor* Michael O'Neill rightly insists that the

10 See *POS*, p. 449.

11 *Shelley's Poetry and Prose*, selected and ed. Donald H. Reiman and Sharon
B. Powers, Norton Critical Editions (New York and London, 1977), p. 473.

12 The most developed of Shelley's examples of this shadow side of psychic
experience is in the figure of the maniac in 'Julian and Maddalo': see my 'The
Shelleyan Psycho-Drama: "Julian and Maddalo" ', *Essays on Shelley*, ed.
Miriam Allott (Liverpool, 1982), pp. 84–90.

work 'involves itself in murkiness, unsureness, exploration'.[13] This queries not only Wasserman's over-schematic approach but also equally influential studies along moralistic lines, such as that by Evan K. Gibson who sees as the poem's central theme 'the temptation of the idealist to live a solitary life rather than find partial ideals of love and companionship in this present world'.[14] Interpreters like Gibson take their cue above all from Shelley's Preface, which undoubtedly finds room for a didactic reading of the fate of the young Poet who 'images to himself the Being whom he loves' and goes in pursuit of the 'vision in which he embodies his own imaginations':[15] the second paragraph opens with a comment on 'The Poet's self-centred seclusion . . . avenged by the furies of an irresistible passion' (POS 463). Yet this promise of a tale of self-absorption and retribution does not erase the impression of the protagonist's nobility in seeking a 'conception' that 'unites all of wonderful, or wise, or beautiful, which the poet, the philosopher, or the lover could depicture' (POS 462). Indeed, the Poet remains one of 'the luminaries of the world', and Shelley reserves his real scorn for another class of men, whose apartness consists in cold-hearted aloofness – 'deluded by no generous error, instigated by no sacred thirst of doubtful knowledge, duped by no illustrious superstition, loving nothing on this earth, and cherishing no hopes beyond' (POS 463). Though Shelley may here be aiming a blow at the apostate author of The Excursion, as well as more generally at the Tory Establishment responsible for the White Terror and for restoring the monarchies after Waterloo, he draws a positive energy from an earlier text by Wordsworth, 'Lines Left upon a Seat in a Yew-tree', first published in Lyrical Ballads (1798), which weaves an appeal for 'benevolence' out of the history of one of 'No common soul', who, withdrawing from his fellow-men, falls victim to an 'unfruitful life' and 'visionary views'.[16] Shelley transfers the epithet 'unfruitful' to the 'self-

---

[13] Michael O'Neill, The Human Mind's Imaginings: Conflict and Achievement in Shelley's Poetry (Oxford, 1989), p. 12.

[14] Evan K. Gibson, 'Alastor: A Reinterpretation', in Shelley's Poetry and Prose, ed. Reiman and Powers, p. 568; reprinted from PMLA, lxii (1947), 1022–42. See also, C. E. Pulos, The Deep Truth: A Study of Shelley's Scepticism (1954; Lincoln, Nebr., 1962), p. 81.

[15] POS, p. 462. All references to Shelley's 'Preface' are from this edition and hereafter bracketed in the text.

[16] 'Lines Left upon a Seat in a Yew-tree', ll. 13, 32, 45. For suggestive pointers to the detailed influence of this poem on Alastor, see POS, p. 459.

ish, blind' men of the world, and his advocacy of humane feeling
extends, even more than does Wordsworth's, to a respect for his 'pure
and tender-hearted' solitary, though, as the words 'deluded', 'doubtful'
and 'duped' indicate, he is ever mindful of the latter's propensity for
error. The Poet is thus irreducibly both cautionary spectacle and
sympathetic hero; in relation to him the Preface solicits esteem, pity
and critical judgement and will not decide between them. The effect
of this is not simply to show Shelley to be in two or three minds, but to
challenge circumscribed habits of mind, be they rigidly moralistic or
otherwise ungenerous. The Preface affirms a liberal ideology of reading, encouraging a full involvement, experiential, analytical and principled, in the poem's presentation of 'one of the most interesting
situations of the human mind' (POS 462).

This ideology reflects a maturity won in the course of writing
Alastor, which is as it were cast back, not unproblematically, upon the
existing poem. The 'interesting situation' that we first encounter in
the text is that of a poet reaching for his credentials in a more basic act
of self-definition:

> Mother of this unfathomable world!
> Favour my solemn song, for I have loved
> Thee ever, and thee only; I have watched
> Thy shadow, and the darkness of thy steps,
> And my heart ever gazes on the depth
> Of thy deep mysteries. I have made my bed
> In charnels and on coffins, where black death
> Keeps record of the trophies won from thee,
> Hoping to still these obstinate questionings
> Of thee and thine, by forcing some lone ghost
> Thy messenger, to render up the tale
> Of what we are.   (ll. 18–29)

However much Wasserman may talk of a Wordsworthian Narrator, the
utterance remains all Shelley's. The whole opening segment of Alastor
(ll. 1–49) is a process of biblio-selving, a becoming in words, in which
the young Shelley strives, while he can, to establish a poetic identity
that is distinctly his own – and in fact does so by pointing his *difference
from* Wordsworth. Shelley's relations with Nature are altogether
darker and more risky than those of his predecessor.[17] Indeed, whereas

17 See O'Neill, pp. 14–16.

Wordsworth's 'natural piety' in 'My heart leaps up' signifies an abiding interaction between self and an external organic reality, in the first section of Shelley's address (ll. 1–17), where the phrase is quoted, Nature seems to have no actual presence at all, for the aesthetic and strongly erotic terms of the prosopopoeic description – 'dewy morn', 'gorgeous ministers', 'midnight's tingling silentness', 'autumn's hollow sighs', 'spring's voluptuous pantings' and 'sweet kisses' – suggest the imagery of dream-vision and longings of an isolate mind. Reaching out for communion with the 'beloved brotherhood' of earth, ocean and air (l. 1), he realizes instead a piquant subjectivity. The lines to 'Mother of this unfathomable world' themselves express, moreover, an involvement in the supernatural rather than the natural. The 'obstinate questionings / Of sense and outward things' for which thanks are given in Wordsworth's 'Immortality Ode' (ll. 142–43) bear witness to a primal imaginative power independent of Nature, yet the intuition of that power's survival is part of a therapeutic process which keeps faith with responsiveness to the miracles of the commonplace, 'splendour in the grass', 'glory in the flower'. Shelley's 'questionings' (l. 26), on the other hand, are an insatiable craving for knowledge of the mystery 'Of what we are', and in this he reproduces a stance of which Wordsworth heartily disapproved, for this paragraph of *Alastor* is closely based upon the account in *The Excursion* (III. 680–705)[18] of the 'perilous way' of the Solitary, who, destitute at his wife's passing, makes unreasonable trial of 'dreams and visions', speaks to 'the grave' and conjures 'Eternity, as men constrain a ghost / To appear and answer' in search of that which is 'veiled from waking thought' – the meaning of life and death. Shelley pushes to an extreme his imaginative commitment to that which Wordsworth reproves out of a belief in the unextravagant well-being of minds 'wedded to this goodly universe / In love and holy passion' (Preface to 1814 *Excursion*, ll. 53–54). Over against Wordsworth's guiding philosophy of 'weddedness' he sets the heterodox attractions of rapacious interrogation, uniting 'breathless kisses' with 'strange tears', 'awful talk' with 'asking looks', attempting 'Such magic as compels the charmèd night / To render up thy charge' (ll. 31–37) in a configuration half of assault and half of seductive cajoling.

---

[18] All references to *The Excursion* are from *The Poetical Works of William Wordsworth*, Volume V, ed. E. de Selincourt and Helen Darbishire, Oxford English Texts (1949; Oxford, 1972).

Occult and sensuous encounter, not 'holy passion', is Shelley's characteristic signature.

Shelley's lines develop then a highly individual posture that is in a
sense anti-Wordsworthian. Yet that posture itself is not a secure one,
and is marked by disturbing ambiguities. We have seen already a
tension between desire for community with external reality and the
claims of self-enclosed oneiric experience, and in the concluding lines
of the induction the same desire is hard-pressed by evocations of
helplessness and neglect:

> though ne'er yet
> Thou hast unveiled thy inmost sanctuary,
> Enough from incommunicable dream,
> And twilight phantasms, and deep noonday thought,
> Has shone within me, that serenely now
> And moveless, as a long-forgotten lyre
> Suspended in the solitary dome
> Of some mysterious and deserted fane,
> I wait thy breath, Great Parent, that my strain
> May modulate with murmurs of the air,
> And motions of the forests and the sea,
> And voice of living beings, and woven hymns
> Of night and day, and the deep heart of man.   (ll. 37–49)

Wordsworth's famous enactment of his 'sense sublime / Of something
far more deeply interfused' ('Tintern Abbey', ll. 93–102) becomes
anticlimax – a set of halting formulations (the alliteration and asson-
ance particularly are strained) indicative of vague, improbable hopes.
What *is* authentic – paradoxicallly so in view of the assertion of
serenity – is the eerie, dry atmosphere of dereliction and stasis. The
jaws of denial tighten in these closing lines: the dream is of breaking
out into the rhythms and sounds of the natural world, but the experience is of being shut up in a small corner of the universe, unsure
whether anything will happen. In this configuration of enclosure,
where the confines are those of the mind, we see a troubled version of
an 'existentialist' position that runs through Shelley's career and
insists on the individual's capacity to go on creating in an alien world
– 'to hope till Hope creates / From its own wreck the thing it contem-
plates' (*Prometheus Unbound*, IV. 573–74). The subsequent account of
the Poet's journeyings and death is, as we shall see, very much
concerned with the possibilities and the problems of that position.
Already, however, the invocation itself has been fraught with a sense

of overarching limitation: even the supernatural can offer up no more than a 'tale' of 'what we are' (ll. 28–29); for better or for worse, we are bound to fictions. The reference to failure – Nature's 'inmost sanctuary' remains screened off from the poet – and to the rather questionable gains of 'twilight phantasms' casts a critical light that recalls the statement in the Preface about being 'duped by . . . illustrious superstition'. Biblio-selving does not exclude instability or self-deprecation. The latter are part and parcel of the way that in *Alastor*, as Michael O'Neill puts it, 'Shelley's self-examining imagination . . . projects figures, narrative situations, and images in an attempt to body forth its obscurest impulses and to see them as other'.[19]

What the story of the Poet's early life and travels most strikingly bodies forth is the desire for ideal states of insight and repose. His youthful wanderings among the ruins of ancient civilizations repeat the Narrator's reaching for knowledge of 'what we are' – except that the Poet's researches are successful, as, poring on the 'speechless shapes' on the walls around him, he 'gazed, till meaning on his vacant mind / Flashed like strong inspiration, and he saw / The thrilling secrets of the birth of time' (ll. 126–28). This image of perfect contemplation, where meaning comes uncalled to the receptive mind, throws into relief the uncertainties and relative blindness of our own, and the poet's, adventures in interpretation; and similarly, the Poet's interaction with Nature, where even the 'wild antelope' would 'suspend / Her timid steps to gaze upon a form / More graceful than her own' (ll. 104–06), evokes a prelapsarian harmony to which the ordinary world is a chaos. Even here we cannot quite escape ambivalence. Do these passages represent situations of productiveness or of stasis? Do the Poet's experiences lead anywhere? All in all, however, the first stages of the Poet's history are the locus of a plenitude of which we dream. Moreover, Shelley's mind operates here in terms of a positive model of development – based upon the biography of the Wanderer in Book I of *The Excursion*. As the Wanderer was reared through contact with Nature and 'In dreams, in study, and in ardent thought' (I. 301–02), so Shelley's Poet was nurtured by 'solemn vision, and bright silver dream' and, 'sent' the 'choicest impulses' of earth and air, drank deep from the 'fountains of divine philosophy'. The pattern is of maturation grounded in special dispensations and an answering energetic dedication.

19 O'Neill, p. 16.

Shelley adopts this structure, however, only to turn it upside-down. Already we have learned (ll. 51–66) that the Poet has sung in 'solitude' and met an 'untimely' death – whereas the Wanderer enjoys a long purposeful life as itinerant teacher and spokesman for a whole range of values, including the definite consolation that he incants over the grave of Margaret at the end of Book I of *The Excursion*. But it is not only the premature ending and relative pointlessness of the Poet's existence that matter: the more striking difference between the two figures lies in their interior make-up, for in contrast to the Wanderer's 'equipoise', 'steady course' and cheerfulness that renders him immune to 'painful pressure from within' (*Excursion*, I. 347–81) the Poet's destiny is to be subject to 'restless impulse' (l. 304). There are at least two journeys in *Alastor*: the developmental model gives way to a narrative of the self driven literally to death on a tide of passion. The turning point comes with the Poet's vision of a 'veilèd maid':

> Her voice was like the voice of his own soul
> Heard in the calm of thought; its music long,
> Like woven sounds of streams and breezes, held
> His inmost sense suspended in its web
> Of many-coloured woof and shifting hues.
> Knowledge and truth and virtue were her theme,
> And lofty hopes of divine liberty,
> Thoughts the most dear to him, and poesy,
> Herself a poet. . . .
>   . . . at the sound he turned,
> And saw by the warm light of their own life
> Her glowing limbs beneath the sinuous veil
> Of woven wind, her outspread arms now bare,
> Her dark locks floating in the breath of night,
> Her beamy bending eyes, her parting lips
> Outstretched, and pale, and quivering eagerly.
> His strong heart sunk and sickened with excess
> Of love. . . .
>   . . . she drew back a while,
> Then, yielding to the irresistible joy,
> With frantic gesture and short breathless cry
> Folded his frame in her dissolving arms.
>   (ll. 153–61, 174–82, 184–87)

Shelley's rejection of the Wanderer as exemplar of selfhood and poethood continues his anti-Wordsworthian polemic and struggle for an alternative wisdom and creativity – a process that will be sustained to the very end of *Alastor*. Yet the above-quoted passage makes specially clear the unguarded input into the poetic process from his private mental places. Mrs O. W. Campbell has a telling remark: 'she who should have been but a symbol of the soul's desire steps out of the land of imagery like some scantily dressed beauty of a society ball'.[20] The passage is dominated by an eroticism, or rather autoeroticism, that disturbs and intrigues, and is far in excess of any sensuous component necessary to complete the epipsyche to which Shelley refers in the Preface as a three-fold creation of 'the intellectual faculties, the imagination, the functions of sense' (*POS* 462). Taking issue with William Keach's view of *Alastor* as exclusively a repository of 'self-inclosed psychical experience', Michael O'Neill argues that the impact even of these lines is irresolvably balanced between 'reflexiveness' and an 'otherness' belonging to the art of mimetic narrative; and certainly he is right to ask, for example, whether the 'like' of 'Her voice was like the voice of his own soul' separates or unites the voices, or whether the phrase 'by the warm light of their own life' does not so much interiorize the light in the mind of the perceiver as stress the objective existence of the 'glowing limbs'.[21] But O'Neill's objection becomes irrelevant if we see the mingling of reflexiveness and otherness, wish-full fantasy and impressions of actuality, as a property of (to use another of Keach's phrases) 'projected self-reflection'.[22] The projection is at one level the protagonist's dream, as is nicely underlined at the end by the double meaning of 'dissolving' (l. 187), which suggests both the fading of the vision and its power to generate sensation; but Shelley's own sensibility is of course implicated in the event – not least a preoccupation with watching, which reaches a climax in the close-up of the imaginary woman's 'parted lips / Outstretched . . . and quivering' and her 'panting . . . frantic' embrace. The mind's eye becomes an organ of intense, though transient, pleasure.

The same effect is present in the preceding passage (ll. 129–39), which describes how an Arab maiden 'watched' the Poet's nightly sleep 'to gaze upon his lips / Parted in slumber' and, 'not daring . . . / To speak her love', returned home 'wildered, and wan, and panting'.

---

[20] O. W. Campbell, *Shelley and the Unromantics* (London, 1924), p. 190.
[21] William Keach, *Shelley's Style* (New York and London, 1984), p. 82; O'Neill, pp. 18–20.
[22] Keach, p. 82.

These lines are often seen as explaining the Poet's subsequent suffering: the daemon of endless longing punishes him for rejecting the
self-abnegating love of a real person. And it is at this point that the
text does seem to encourage moralizing interpretation, in the comment that the Poet is one who 'spurned' the 'choicest gifts' of 'sweet
human love' (ll. 203–05). Yet this perspective is offered only to be
exposed as a false imposition of authority, since the Poet can hardly
have 'spurned' the maiden's devotion if she never admitted it (ll.
133–34). As products of Shelley's imagination (or, for that matter, a
Narrator's) the two episodes are in parallel rather than enacting a
sequence of crime and retribution: the imagery of the veilèd maid's
beauty and frenzied yielding repeats from a different angle the same
sensuous obsession as is constituted by that of the Arab maiden's
excited gaze and feverish dereliction.

Roland Barthes, adapting Freud, celebrates narrative as that which
allows us to 'transcend the first *form* given man, namely repetition'; it
is an emancipatory logic 'which has vanquished repetition and in-
stituted the model of the process of becoming'.[23] What is most radical
about the treatment of the human mind in *Alastor* is that it bears
manifest witness to the might of the immature 'first form' itself, which
it sets over against the adult 'form' which is narrative and the drama of
inward development. The recurrent word pictures of watching and
being watched, or of sexual encounter, are part of a larger pattern
whereby local intensities, psychodramatic or catching life in a symbolic attitude, usurp the forwards thrust of events and meaning.
Another example comes immediately that the Poet awakens from his
dream in the 'cold white light of morning, the blue moon / Low in the
west, the clear and garish hills', and 'His wan eyes / Gaze on the empty
scene as vacantly / As ocean's moon looks on the moon in heaven' (ll.
192–202). The chill, the blank distinctness, the sinking, the emptiness
are at once properties of the outer scene and symptoms of the Poet's
desolation; his vacant gaze is the reverse – the mirror image – of the
fullness of his dream: the text rests as it were upon his arrested interior
life. This fore-coming of inner states persists throughout the Poet's
subsequent journey, to which we must now turn. It is worth noting,
however, that the whole of that journey is in a sense an antinarrative,

---

[23] Roland Barthes, 'Introduction to the Structural Analysis of Narratives',
Barthes: Image-Music-Text, essays selected and translated by Stephen Heath
(London, 1977), p. 124.

and an antitype of the 'process of becoming'. *Alastor* records in the final analysis a process of *unbecoming*: its *telos*, or appointed end, is death, and the Poet seems to exist for the sake of his dissolution. There is at one point in the text a salient self-interpreting moment that actually denies the importance of how or why the the Poet's journey came about, or whether it was self-inflicted or directed by some external force:

> The meeting boughs and implicated leaves
> Wove twilight o'er the Poet's path, as led
> By love, or dream, or god, or mightier Death,
> He sought in Nature's dearest haunt, some bank,
> Her cradle, and his sepulchre.   (ll. 426–30)

What ultimately matters is not cause or reason but the still point where the destination of the individual life – 'his sepulchre' – meets Nature's originary source – 'Her cradle'. In this idea of the organism feeding a greater organic unity there may be an 'emancipatory logic' of a sort – especially for one who, like Shelley, thought he might be dying.

Before this, however, comes the journey itself, which embodies Shelley's dark vision of existence as constant subjection to tyranny from within. The register is set by the formal simile of the eagle grasped by the serpent (ll. 227–32), who 'feels her breast / Burn with the poison': the Poet's 'lovely dream' becomes a consuming passion, not only urging him blindly onwards but gradually destroying the life that 'shone / As in a furnace burning secretly from his dark eyes alone' (ll. 252–54). Entrapment and smouldering fire remain the dominant images, and, though they may suggest struggle and persistence as well as pressure and decay, the emphasis falls firmly on the negative side. There are moments of hope and aspiration, as when the Poet is prompted by the flight of the dying swan to think of the joys that may await him in the unseen world: if the bird sings sweet notes prophesying reunion with 'eyes / Bright in the lustre of their own fond joy', why should he, whose spirit is 'more vast' and 'more attuned to beauty', linger in a dimension of 'deaf air' and 'blind earth' beneath a heaven that 'echoes not [his] thoughts' (ll. 280–90). The Poet discovers that the idea of sympathy between man and nature is but an illusion, and that fulfilment lies beyond this world. But the advance in this of course is more apparent than real: the satisfactions of the immortal realm may be themselves illusory, as his own intuitions tell him, for death is 'Faithless perhaps as sleep' – a 'shadowy lure, / With doubtful smile mocking its own strange charms' (ll. 294–95). The bid for freedom through thought ends only in felt confinement; the wings of transcendence get stuck in the trap of uncertainty – and of returning obsession, the imagined 'lure' of death being remarkably like that of a seductive woman.

As in 'O! there are spirits', the positives of Romantic 'philosophy' – oneness with Nature and imagination as a means of grace – are thus exposed as constructs and found wanting. Romance and myth are similarly called in question, so much so that they become the ingredients almost of a comedy of errors. The Poet exults in the buoyancy that sweeps him across the ocean amidst the 'fearful war' of blast and wave –

> As if their genii were the ministers
> Appointed to conduct him to the light
> Of those beloved eyes, the Poet sate
> Holding the steady helm.   (ll. 330–33)

But a definite shadow of doubt is cast by the 'As if', so that we experience the Poet's 'rejoicing' (l. 325) as subjective reaction – as, that is, speculative fiction and potential misconception. The figure of the epic adventurer is menaced by irony, and this effect is intensified by the Poet's own cry:

> 'Vision and Love!'
> The Poet cried aloud, 'I have beheld
> The path of thy departure. Sleep and death
> Shall not divide us long!'   (ll. 366–69)

For Michael O'Neill this exemplifies 'the poem's element of immaturity . . . beacuse the lines have a blurb's simplifying crudity'.[24] In fact, the crudity is the poem's subtlety, for it belongs all to the Poet and points the blindness of his visionary desire as he utters a premature celebration against the threatening background of 'crags [that] closed round with black and jagged arms' (l. 359) and a 'cavern there [that] / Yawned' (ll. 363–64) – not the embrace and quivering mouth of a Lover, but the arms and the jaws of grim Death.

Landscape often functions to ironize the Poet's situation and frame

[24] O'Neill, p. 24.

of mind. The very boat on which he embarks to the regions of Death images his incipient disintegration, for 'its sides / Gaped wide with many a rift, and its frail joints / Swayed with the undulations of the tide' (ll. 301–03); and when we hear that it 'Safely fled' the tempest 'As if that frail and wasted human form / Had been an elemental god' (ll. 349–51) the conditional mood again undercuts the mythopoeic treatment of the protagonist, leaving us with an irresolvable impression of the Poet as both hero and fool. It is at this point, moreover, when the Poet comes upon a tranquil cove, that his surroundings yield their most explicit comment upon his inner state, for here 'yellow flowers / For ever gaze on their own drooping eyes, / Reflected in the crystal calm' (ll. 406–08): we are pressed to see in the Poet that archetypal species of self-absorption, narcissism.

But Shelley does not stop there, with the Poet a tragicomical hero-victim in a drama of self-delusion. There is a second turning point in the journey which signalizes a genuine advance in perception on the Poet's part and represents Shelley's incipient grasp of a philosophy to live by, an adequate private ontology. The advance comes not in the acquisition of knowledge, nor in a Romantic capacity for transcendence, but in the acceptance of uncertainty:

> 'O stream!
> Whose source is inaccessibly profound,
> Whither do thy mysterious waters tend?
> Thou imagest my life. Thy darksome stillness,
> Thy dazzling waves, thy loud and hollow gulfs,
> Thy searchless fountain, and invisible course
> Have each their type in me: and the wide sky,
> And measureless ocean may declare as soon
> What oozy cavern or what wandering cloud
> Contains thy waters, as the universe
> Tell where these living thoughts reside, when stretched
> Upon thy flowers my bloodless limbs shall waste
> I'the passing wind!'   (ll. 502–14)

In Lloyd Abbey's view, this soliloquy of the Poet looks towards the metaphysical perspective of 'Mont Blanc': though he does not see 'the existential interdependence' of mind and stream, he does approach this awareness in his realization that the flow of the stream typifies the flow of his perceptions; and the One Life philosophy of 'Mont Blanc' is anticipated in the fact that 'Ocean and sky are macrocosm to the stream in the same way "the universe" is macrocosm to the poet's "living thoughts" '.[25] Certainly there is a depth of suggestiveness in the passage that is quite absent from its probable source in *The Excursion* (III. 967–91), where the stream is used simply as a metaphor for the perplexing onwards rush of life to an 'unfathomable gulf' into whose stillness the despondent Solitary hopes soon to descend; and that suggestiveness undoubtedly evokes Shelley's later wrestlings with concepts of an ineffable universal Power and its relations, as Prime Mover, to the individual mind (which seems to be at once informed by it and freed into autonomous creativity by its indifference to the human condition). Yet what is most significant within the context of *Alastor* itself is the Poet's wide-awake embrace of his state of ignorance: the words 'inaccessibly', 'mysterious', 'darksome', 'searchless', 'invisible', 'measureless' all emphasize that the secrets of the universe are unknowable, while the closing lines express an equally strong sense that there can be no sure answers to questions of the origins or ends of human thought or existence. The Poet's prospect of his bodily wasting against a background of beauty and growth (the flowers) in 'the passing wind' implies, moreover, his apprehension of a permanence to which his own life is but a passing show: he knows that his thoughts are 'living' and that nature lives, but there is no guarantee that the former are anything more than transient – than coterminous with physical being. There is no reaching here for immortality.

The Poet's openness to an unknown future and to the macrocosmic 'flow' of nature indicates, then, a new wisdom and stability. Thereafter the whole tenor of the journey alters, taking on a more active and yet more peaceful aura: 'Calm, he still pursued the stream' (ll. 539–40); he is ready to meet Death without any concern for what that encounter might mean or bring. The catharsis is both the Poet's and Shelley's own, and it is impossible at times to distinguish between the former's mental experience and the latter's projection of a more affirmative perspective on the world and being-in-the-world. Thus, the landscape which had once reflected the Poet's longing and shut-in state – the 'eyes' of parasite blossoms 'Fold their beams round the hearts of those that love' and 'twine their tendrils with the wedded boughs / Uniting their close union' (ll. 443–45)[26] – now allegorizes an imperceptible

[25] Lloyd Abbey, *Destroyer and Preserver: Shelley's Poetic Skepticism* (Lincoln, Nebr. and London, 1979), p. 28.
[26] There are comparable landscapes in the best-known long poem of the late eighteenth century, Cowper's *The Task*, but in that work the plants which are

process of change where life is not so much driven to consume itself as painlessly withdrawn:

> so from his steps
> Bright flowers departed, and the beautful shade
> Of the green groves, with all their odorous winds
> And musical motions.   (ll. 536–39)

Death belongs after all, it seems, to a universal order that is essentially benign – an impression subsequently enforced not only by reference to the nurturing of life in the 'silent nook' of decay (ll. 571–600), where the stones are covered with ivy 'for ever green' and the mould nurses 'rainbow flowers', but, more curiously, in the abrupt invocation to Death (ll. 609–24) which, while recognizing the 'devastation' wrought on earth from the 'red field' of slaughter to the 'snowy bed' of innocence, predicts a time when the world's rulers (a 'regal prey') will themselves be destroyed and men will die natural deaths 'like flowers or creeping worms'. The single image which has most obvious bearing upon the Poet's predicament in this section of the poem also unites realism and aspiration: the 'pine' which 'stretched athwart the vacancy / Its swinging boughs' (ll. 561–63), emblem of survival in the face of adversity, imparts a certain glamour to the Poet's last wanderings, as does the depiction of his deathbed recollections, in his 'high and holy soul', of 'the majestic past' (ll. 627–32). This account of the Poet's looking back prevents any implication that he is united with his vision. The effect, however, is not, as Evan K. Gibson would have it, to insist upon 'the danger of neglecting love and sympathy with one's fellow-man in this life',[27] but rather to highlight the protagonist's freedom from the grip of his passion. As death approaches, 'Hope and despair, / The torturers, slept' (639–40). This is Shelley's dream of how death will come – nobly, romantically, as release and as repose.

But *does* the Poet find freedom? The last passage of the narrative is also its most ambiguous:

'wedded . . . like beauty to old age, / For int'rest sake, the living to the dead', or whose 'clasping tendrils' recompense 'the strength they borrow with the grace they lend' (see *Task*, III. 657–74) symbolize an optimal social order and so throw into relief Shelley's contrasting concern with subjective states. The entwinings in *Alastor* signify at once the Poet's desire for 'union' and the parasitical grip that desire has upon him.
27 Gibson, p. 564.

>   his last sight
> Was the great moon, which o'er the western line
> Of the wide world her mighty horn suspended, . . .
> And when two lessening points of light alone
> Gleamed through the darkness, the alternate gasp
> Of his faint respiration scarce did stir
> The stagnate night: – till the minutest ray
> Was quenched, the pulse still lingered in his heart.
> It paused – it fluttered. But when heaven remained
> Utterly black, the murky shades involved
> An image, silent, cold, and motionless,
> As their own voiceless earth and vacant air.
> Even as a vapour fed with golden beams
>   . . . was now that wondrous frame –
> No sense, no motion, no divinity –
> A fragile lute, on whose harmonious strings
> The breath of heaven did wander – a bright stream
> Once fed with many-voicèd waves – a dream
> Of youth, which night and time have quenched for ever,
> Still, dark, and dry, and unremembered now.
>   (ll. 645–47, 654–63, 665–71)

This takes us back in a long arc to the point just before the soliloquy beside the stream. Peering into a 'well', a 'liquid mirror', the Poet's 'eyes beheld / Their own wan light through the reflected lines / Of his thin hair' (ll. 469–71); the Spirit of nature – 'woods' and 'leaping rivulet' – 'Held commune with him', only to be replaced in his 'regard' by 'two eyes':

>   Two starry eyes, hung in the gloom of thought,
>   And seemed with their serene and azure smiles
>   To beckon him.   (ll. 490–92)

As the Poet's life ebbs away, Shelley reactivates these earlier configurations of reflection and reflexiveness. William Keach comments that the Poet once again sees his own eyes 'duplicated', this time by the still visible tips of the crescent moon, but that this continuance of 'the poem's ambiguous merging of introspective and projective vision' takes a climactic turn as the Poet becomes in death merely an 'image' in the void that surrounds him: we become aware of an overarching perception – that of the narrator – 'which includes . . . the wandering poet as the object of its own reflexive perception'.[28] This reading is

---

[28] Keach, pp. 85–86.

supported by the fact it is impossible to decide whether the 'two lessening points of light' (l. 654) are aspects of the Poet himself, already condensed into 'image', or of the moon he looks at. Yet the detail also plainly evokes the 'starry eyes' of the dream-maiden, suggesting that the obsession is still after all in place, exerting an ineradicable power and again usurping the impressions of nature's own phenomena. (It is hardly plausible to claim, as the editors of Shelley do, that the two points of light simply 'replace' the eyes 'that have hitherto obsessed him'.)[29] The words 'remained' (l. 661) and 'heart' (l. 658) are important: the Poet even now waits for something to happen, and so long as the light gleams through the darkness there is still both life and longing within him; when heaven stays 'black' the lingering pulse of hope and being dies. For the last time his expectations are disappointed.

The picture of the Poet cruelly mystified to the very end, in spite of the apparently liberating recognitions of the stream soliloquy, issues a raw jolt and lesson in human vulnerability. On another level, however, it initiates a complicating and deepening of the poem's wisdom, which ultimately shares in both the tragic implications of the Poet's story and the philosophic insights of the soliloquy itself. Though it is convenient to speak, as Keach does, of a 'narrator', that Shelley *is* palpably at work, forging and promulgating such a wisdom, becomes obvious in the light of his return to a perceptible dialogue with Wordsworth. The final movement of *Alastor* is plainly written out of its author's reaction to the tragedy he alludes to by quotation in his Preface: the 'sore heart-wasting' of Margaret in *The Excursion* (I. 875).

Shelley's repetition (ll. 658–59) of Wordsworth's key words 'heart', 'lingered' and 'remained' ('nine long years, / She lingered in unquiet widowhood; / . . . one torturing hope . . . / Fast rooted at her heart: and here, my Friend, – / In sickness she remained' (I. 872–73, 913–15)) suggests that he has Wordsworth's text firmly in mind, although the surrealistic quality of his scene distinguishes it sharply from his predecessor's understated treatment of Margaret's tragedy of self-delusion – her slow decay under the burden of unsatisfied longing for her husband's return, as 'evermore her eye / Was busy in the distance, shaping things / That made her heart beat quick' (I. 880–82). There is a mixture of painfulness and calm in both accounts, compounded in Shelley by the final gathering up (ll. 667–70) of earlier motifs into the .

---

[29] POS, p. 487.

taut, precarious equipoise of elegiac inscription – the 'fragile lute' that
is silent (recalling the concept of poet as wind-harp at ll. 41–49), the
'bright stream' now run 'dry' (recalling ll. 494–514), and the 'dream of
youth' that lies 'unremembered'. This last reference recollects not
only, as Shelley's editors assume,[30] the vision of the veiled maiden, a
'dream of hopes' (ll. 149–51), but also the designation of the Poet as
'lovely youth' (l. 55): the haunting vision may thankfully have been
forgotten in death, but so too is the Poet 'unremembered'. The disconcerting sense of death as the premature terminus of potentiality – of
something 'quenched for ever' – challenges Michael O'Neill's reading
of the lines as communicating 'an end to fretting over unanswerable
questions'.[31] There is a definite residue of nagging resentment at the
impositions of 'night and time', which then flares up dramatically in
the narrator's closing address. Shelley's point is that we cannot help
but 'fret' in the face of suffering and loss, that we *should* 'fret', and that
it is Wordsworth's lamentable failing at the end of Book I of *The
Excursion* that he tries to persuade his readers not to 'fret'.

The closing address of *Alastor* (ll. 672–720) begins with invocations
to the sorceress Medea, who raised the dead by 'wondrous alchemy', to
God, who conferred immortality (revengefully) upon Ahasuerus, the
Wandering Jew, and to the ancient alchemists with their dream of
discovering an *elixir vitae*. These are but desperate gestures, for the
Poet, 'The brave, the gentle, and the beautiful, / The child of grace
and genius', is irrecoverably gone – 'hast fled'. The appeal to magic
and occult science, however, reminds us of the gothic manoeuvres at
the outset of the poem, where Shelley had established a poetic voice
in contradistinction to that of Wordsworth; and in the parting lament
the older poet is again evoked as the precursor who is being struggled
against and corrected. As a postscript to the Preface Shelley had
introduced lines from *The Excursion* (I. 500–02: the slight mis-
quotation is neither here nor there): 'The good die first, / And those
whose hearts are dry as summer dust, / Burn to the socket' (POS 463).
He keeps faith with the sentiment of this in his conclusion, setting the
demise of the harmless Poet against the background of a world in
which 'Heartless things / Are done and said . . . and many worms /
And beasts and men live on', but in doing so he presses a humane
viewpoint which, as we saw from the sonnet 'To Wordsworth', he felt

[30] POS, p. 487.
[31] O'Neill, p. 28.

Wordsworth had to all intents and purposes abandoned, and then moves on to query the whole consolatory outlook of the Wanderer's speech to the young poet at the end of Book I of *The Excursion*, which blends comforting references to Margaret's peace after death in the bosom of Nature with reminders of the support always to be found through active meditation (*Excursion*, I. 939–56). The speech is continually echoed to be denied: the 'vesper low and joyous orison' of 'mighty Earth' that recall the religious atmosphere surrounding the spot where Margaret passed away are no solace in face of the simple compulsive recognition, thrice repeated (ll. 686, 688, 695), that the Poet is 'fled'; the atheistical Shelley's Providence is no repository of the 'purposes of wisdom' (*Excursion*, I. 933) but one 'Profuse of poisons' coupled with the pagan figure of Medea; the 'tranquillity, / So calm and still' which composes the Wanderer's 'uneasy thoughts' (I. 946–48) becomes the 'cold tranquillity' that Shelley's Poet leaves disturbingly behind (l. 717); the Wanderer's confidence that despair arising from transience – that is, from 'ruin and . . . change' – and the grief arising from the 'passing shows of Being' are but an 'idle dream' that cannot dominate the 'enlightened spirit' (I. 949–55) has no place in Shelley's vision of a universe whose 'phantasmal scene' is significant not so much because it is unreal in comparison with some higher order of truth but simply because it survives the Poet who is 'not' (ll. 696–99).

For Shelley, all forms of elegy are but empty tropes, 'speak[ing] in feeble imagery / Their own cold powers' (ll. 709–10); when he advises, like Wordsworth's Wanderer, 'Let no tear be shed' (ll. 702–03: compare *Excursion*, I. 932, 940) it is not because there are reasons to cheer up but because he knows that it is pointless in the face of the surpassing reality of mortality and change:

> Art and eloquence,
> And all the shows o'the world are frail and vain
> To weep a loss that turns their lights to shade.
> It is a woe 'too deep for tears,' when all
> Is reft at once, when some surpassing Spirit,
> Whose light adorned the world around it, leaves
> Those who remain behind, not sobs or groans,
> The passionate tumult of a clinging hope;
> But pale despair and cold tranquillity,
> Nature's vast frame, the web of human things,
> Birth and the grave, that are not as they were.
>   (ll. 710–20)

The consolations of *The Excursion* are deconstructed as unavailing
fictions or falsehoods, not a set of inviolable truths. At the same time
the direct quotation from an earlier Wordsworth elevates heart-felt,
inexpressible feelings of bereavement over all expressible compensa-
tions. The only certain knowledge we possess is that things 'are not as
they were' (1. 720). The poem hovers on a double-edged abyss of dumb
despair and stoical acceptance.

There is a wisdom in all of this, the getting of which is a major
aspect of the 'selving' that takes place in *Alastor*. The poem ends in
stasis, but Shelley has discovered, in a modification of the scepticism
of the stream soliloquy, that if any way lies forward it is not through
semi-religious dogma or philosophic notions of a universal harmony
where 'whatever is, is right' but through the knowledge that 'Nature's
vast frame' and 'the web of human things' are separate (as they
saliently are in the phrasing of Shelley's penultimate line) and out of
step one with the other, and through a commitment to creative acts as
a means of surviving that apprehended disharmony and a sense of the
irresistible ritual process of 'Birth and the grave'. He, and we, are
dependent on the 'Art and eloquence' whose efficacy it is easy on one
level to deny. It could be argued that, by a common Romantic alchemy, the poetry of *Alastor* as a whole, not least in its radical explorations of the psychic realm of desire or mis-taking, or in its potent
aestheticizing of death itself, redeems negation as the material of insight and pleasure. In 'brood[ing] over the thoughts and emotions of
his own soul' (to recall Mary Shelley's remarks on the effects of his
ill-health) the poet who thought he was dying wrote his life into a
destiny and into a rich shifting kaleidoscope of feelings and symbolic
landscapes: a point underscored by Mary's often-quoted summary,
whose hagiographic tinge shows her as inheritor of Shelley's bid to
transcend the limits of mortality:

> None of Shelley's poems is more characteristic than this. The
> solemn spirit that reigns throughout, the worship of the majesty of
> nature, the broodings of a poet's heart in solitude – the mingling of
> the exulting joy which the various aspects of the visible universe
> inspires with the sad and struggling pangs which human passion
> imparts – give a touching interest to the whole.[32]

Yet creativity for Shelley at the end of *Alastor* also includes – as the

---

32 'Note on *Alastor*', *PW*, p. 31.

last part to be written, the Preface, emphasizes – a lesson in the claims of 'human sympathy' (*POS* 463). To deny that the poem is the seamless moralistic statement that some critics have made of it is not to say that it is without moral sense. The *Queen Mab*-like indignant scorn against the 'red field . . . the scaffold and the throne' (ll. 614–17) interpolates a reminder that Shelley's idealism was at times trained strenuously outwards upon the contemporary scene in socio-political terms. His opposition in *Alastor* to the Wordsworth of *The Excursion* is itself inevitably a political event – the libertarian's argument with a lost leader – but the grounds of his idealism have moved to a concern with 'being' as opposed to 'belief', understanding rather than doctrine. Transcending extravagant urges, whether in the sphere of the occult or of the erotic, he founds at last a humanized self, feeling though uncertain, trying though not triumphant. *Alastor* represents a critique and personal project firmly rooted in historical and biographical circumstance, but as psychodrama and a mapping of 'human passion' and experience of the world it pleads – ideologically – the primacy of transhistorical interests and values. The wonder is that Shelley was only twenty-three years old when he did all this.

'Ozymandias': The Text in Time

KELVIN EVEREST

I want in this essay to explore a number of questions raised by recent broad trends in literary theory. These trends are towards an emphasis on creativity and freedom in the act of interpretation. The drive is to dispense with the idea of the 'Author' and of authorial intention – authority – and to stress instead the liberated polysemic and many-voiced character of criticism. The sources and elaborations of critical positions of this kind are nowadays very well-known, and need no new rehearsal here. They call into question the status of the text which is the occasion for criticism, by implying that meaning resides more or less exclusively in the interpreting consciousness and its contexts. A refinement of this view has more recently drawn upon developments in the theory of textual criticism strictly conceived – that is, the theory of the editing of texts – to argue that texts materially mutate, inevitably, in the ordinary processes by which they are transmitted through time. This process thereby generates a wealth of diversity and variation in the actual form of any text, which can then be fed back into the critical activity by rendering the object of critical attention literally fluid and indeterminate.[1] New technology, notably the imminent development of computerised 'hypertext' editions which bring together all the proliferated variations thrown up in any text by its existence in time, has brought much nearer the possibility of a critical activity which does not simply 'make up' its text in the sense of finding meanings for it, but simultaneously 'makes up' a text on the computer screen which exists simply in relation to the reading offered for it.[2] I wish to enter some questions about these assumptions, and to argue that poems in reality require a kind of intellectual responsibility in

---

[1]   Some of the issues raised by recent developments in the theory of editing are conveniently brought together by Duncan Wu, 'Editing Intentions', *Essays in Criticism* xli (1991), pp. 1–10; this article also briefly notes recent important contributions to the debate, by Jerome McGann, D. F. Mackenzie, Donald H. Reiman, and others.

[2]   For a discussion and exemplification of new possibilities for textual work created by computer applications, see for example Kathryn Sutherland, 'A Guide Through the Labyrinth: Dickens's *Little Dorrit* as Hypertext', *Literary and Linguistic Computing* v (1990), pp. 305–309.

their readers amd their editors which should preclude free play of this kind. I have chosen a simple example from Shelley's poetical canon, although it would certainly be easy to find plenty of extremely complicated examples. 'Ozymandias' offers an accessible case which happens to raise some of the abstract issues itself in the displaced form of its thematic preoccupations and implications.

Shelley's sonnet 'Ozymandias' is undoubtedly amongst the best-known of all his poems. Since the mid-nineteenth century it has been anthologised countless times. Even nowadays, when the place of pre-twentieth century English poetry in any really existent shared national culture is clearly reduced, there is a good chance that most educated people will at least have come across the poem. Its length, and the accessible directness with which its irony appears to work, make it ideal for study in schools. Its form also lends itself to memorisation – as a matter of fact, Shelley's intricate craftsmanship as a writer makes him generally memorable, in the strict sense – so that it forms a part, still, of that body of verse which a literate person will tend to know, whatever their specific tastes and preferences within the English literary tradition. It has, so to speak, survived; it persists beyond the immediate context of its making, like a monument fixed in a setting which has long since changed out of all recognition.

It is puzzling that the sonnet has attracted very little attention from Shelley's commentators.[3] Perhaps it is considered too obvious, or too brief; perhaps it even seems rather uncharacteristic of Shelley's typical

---

[3] Many articles – but very few chapters or even pages in book-length studies – have been published on 'Ozymandias', but almost all of them concentrate on the question of sources. Amongst the best and most persuasive of these are D. W. Thompson, 'Ozymandias', *Philological Quarterly* xvi (1937), pp. 59–64; H. J. Pettit, 'Shelley and Denon's "Voyage Dans La Haute et La Basse Egypte"', *Revue de Littérature Comparée*, xviii (1938), pp. 326–34; J. Gwyn Griffiths, 'Shelley's "Ozymandias" and Diodorus Siculus', *MLR* xliii (1948), pp. 80–84; H. M. Richmond, 'Ozymandias and the Travellers', *KSJ* xi (1962), pp. 65–71; see also briefer discussions by Johnston Parr, 'Shelley's "Ozymandias" Again', *MLR* xlvi (1951), pp. 441–2, and 'Shelley's *Ozymandias*', *KSJ* vi (1957), pp. 31–35, and J. Notopoulos, 'Shelley's "Ozymandias" Once Again', *MLR* xlvii (1953), pp. 442–3. Of possible actual sources that Shelley may have had in mind when composing the poem, the most plausible is Dr Richard Pococke, *A Description of the East and Some Other Countries* (1742; also in volume 10 of J. Pinkerton, *General Collection of Voyages* (1808–1814)), which includes striking illustrations and a number of descriptive passages which accord with details in the poem; see also Dominique Vivant Denon, *Voyage dans la Basse el la Haute Egypte pendant les campagnes du général Bonaparte* (2 volumes, Paris 1802; translated by Arthur Aikin as *Travels in Upper and Lower Egypt . . .*, 3 volumes

styles and habits of mind. But its strategies, even if on the face of it too obvious for comment, will perhaps emerge as more complicated and elusive in the process of being spelt out. It is however first necessary, as a part of the argument I wish to develop, to establish the form of the poem which my critical analysis will address. It is a hybrid form, created by an editor (the present writer):

> I met a traveller from an antique land,
> Who said – 'Two vast and trunkless legs of stone
> Stand in the desert . . . near them, on the sand,
> Half sunk a shattered visage lies, whose frown,
> 5   And wrinkled lip, and sneer of cold command,
> Tell that its sculptor well those passions read
> Which yet survive, stamped on these lifeless things,
> The hand that mocked them, and the heart that fed;
> And on the pedestal these words appear:
> 10 My name is Ozymandias, King of Kings,
> Look on my Works ye Mighty, and despair!
> Nothing beside remains. Round the decay
> Of that colossal Wreck, boundless and bare
> The lone and level sands stretch far away'. –

It's a simple moral. The tyrant's affirmation of his omnipotence, sneeringly arrogant and contemptuous of its human cost, has been ironised by time. The scene reported by the traveller gives the lie unanswerably to the boast on the pedestal; more than that, the scene most tellingly inverts the claims of the legend, 'Look on my Works ye Mighty, and despair!'. Ozymandias's message to posterity has ended up articulating just exactly the opposite to what was intended.

    The poem's grammatical construction subtly reinforces this most emphatic of the poem's first impressions, the unanswerable quality of

[2 volumes in the American edition], 1803); E. Claude Savary, *Letters on Egypt* (English translation, 2 volumes, 1787); Count Volney, *Travels through Syria and Eqypt* . . . (English translation, 3 volumes, 1793); and a number of other works, including Raleigh's *History of the World*, James Bruce's *Travels to Discover the Source of the Nile* (1804), and Robert Walpole's *Memoirs* (1817). But the sonnet's probable inception in the context of a timed competition, and also the evidence of the drafts for the poem in Shelley's notebook (see below, note 11), strongly suggest that Shelley is working imaginatively with materials that were generally current in his literary culture. The rough drafts in the notebook show, for example, that Shelley's first attempts at an opening include no reference to any 'traveller'.

its irony. We feel that the question of tyranny's durability and the
validity of its claims to universal power has been settled absolutely by
what we learn, taken completely beyond argument and debate. It is
simply true that tyranny does not last. The poem's air of dispassion-
ately reporting a simple truth is an effect, in part at least, of the
measured and deliberated movement of the verse. The syntax is, in the
first few lines, entirely that of careful speech, both in the opening line
or so which the poet speaks, and in the studied observations that the
traveller conveys. The marked grammatical pause at the end of the
first line, emphasised with a comma, lends a kind of conviction and
definiteness to the 'Who said' at the beginning of line two; we are
inclined to believe the poet's reporting of what the traveller reports, as
well as the report itself. The provenance is made to seem reliable. The
traveller's own words are shaped into a syntactical and grammatical
sequence which dramatises a careful, almost itemised procedure of
surveying and noting, distantly suggesting the style of British Levantine topographical and early archaeological writings. But this scrupu-
lous listing of features and details – 'near them, on the sand, / Half
sunk . . . lies, . . . frown, / . . . lip, . . . command,' – is slightly modified
by an undercurrent of muted excitement in the description, as of one
reporting a momentous archaeological find. This undercurrent is dis-
cernible in the suspension points which indicate a tensed hiatus in the
narrative ('desert . . . near'), and also in the acceleration of pace in the
first half of the fourth line, achieved by the choice not to punctuate
with a comma (after 'sunk') in a sequence where semantic units are
otherwise consistently so marked: 'Half sunk a shattered visage lies'.

The believable directness of tone, with its implication that the
details of the scene are being specified in a verifiable way, is superseded
in lines 6–8 by a more difficult syntactic organisation, as the traveller's
account moves away from the descriptive manner and into an inter-
pretational idiom. Here we're made to feel the different and more
taxing intellectual demands of teasing a meaning from the monument.
There is room now, even a need, for a way of speaking which suits
ambivalence and difficulty. The sculpted face has features which suggest to the traveller that its maker had accurately interpreted the
generic characteristics of the Tyrant. This prompts a further reflection
on the way that the representation of Ozymandias's 'visage' has long
outlasted both the living human who nourished tyrannical qualities in
his person and conduct, and the living artist who effected the representation (the pronoun 'them' in line eight of course refers to the
'passions' of line six, and this same pronoun is then understood after

'fed'). This is in fact not quite the same irony which we have so far been noting in the sonnet. It is now not simply that Ozymandias's claim to omnipotence has been invalidated by its lone survival in a setting otherwise utterly changed; this irony is compounded and complicated by the additional fact that what has really survived is the artist's skill in representation and interpretation.

These reflections and implications are grammatically compressed, and the syntax suggests that the formal demands of the poem are exerting a pressure on the idiomatic articulacy of the writing. We can note here a first decided instance of the poem's extraordinary capacity to raise without overt statement the relevance of the ostensible subject-matter to its own – that is to say, the poem's – mode of existence. An acknowledgement of the sculptor's consummate and time-defeating skill in representation, fusing local veracity with an image of the human which seems permanently true, is made at a point in the poem which draws attention to its own character as a piece of art, an interpretive representation.

The inverted syntax in line six, for example, 'well those passions read', has perhaps been produced by the demands of the rhyme scheme; although this is not an obvious way to account for it in an actual experience of reading, as the rhyme on 'read' is here introduced for the first time, rather than chiming with an antecedent. Indeed the point makes clear how difficult it is in reality to separate out the various effects of the poem's grammar from those of its formal organisation. The sonnet's opening line, for instance, does not effect its measured and deliberated quality from syntax alone, but from the interplay of metre and rhythm which is at once a form for and a function of paraphraseable sense (that is to say, the rhythm can never be heard unless the sense is also grasped). 'I met a traveller from an antique land,'; the underlying iambic pentameter is gently pulled into a pattern enacting, at the level of rhythm, a calmly controlled and balanced voice. The caesural pause after 'traveller' gives the line a symmetrical disposition of stresses, with the first half ending on two successive weak beats, and the second half commencing with two (there is only a very light stress on 'from'); and the weight of 'met' has its equivalent in the first syllable of 'antique' (which in 1817 would still have been stressed in that way, just as the etymologically cognate 'antic' still is).

The octave of the sonnet is completed in a line which reverts to a similar effect of balanced rhythm within the metre, but with an exaggerated, antithetical emphasis which suggests Pope or even Dryden:

'The hand that mocked them, and the heart that fed;'. The decidedly more difficult intellectual drift of lines 6–8 is thus resolved in a line which at once clarifies the grammar of the sentence ('survive' is revealed as transitive and looking forward to these balanced clauses), and marshalls the complexity and ambivalence of thought to a contained form.

The difficulty of lines 6–8 needs to be understood also in relation to the sonnet's unusual rhymes. Shelley, like Keats during roughly the same period, from early 1817 to late 1819, repeatedly experiments with sonnet form. These experiments involve in particular a straining against the limits of conventional ryhme patterns in the English sonnet tradition, and they culminate in the 'Ode to the West Wind' and in Keats's extraordinary set of variations in the developing stanza forms of the Odes of Spring 1819. 'Ozymandias' has an odd and elusive rhyme scheme: *ababacdcedefef*. There are half-rhymes in lines two and four ('stone' and 'frown'), in line five against lines one and three ('command', 'land', 'sand'), and in lines nine and thirteen ('appear', 'bare'). These combine to make it still more difficult to hear the poem's patterns of rhyme. The patterns are distinguished by a refusal to settle into repeated sequence, while simultaneously hinting at such repetition. There is a broad division into octave and sestet, matching the sense in the manner of the Petrarchan sonnet; but the rhymes on lines seven and ten ('things', 'Kings') knit the two parts together, just as the octave/sestet division is blurred by the possibility that the true 'turn' in the poem's argument may be located in the understated ironic juxtaposition between lines eleven and twelve. In one aspect the ryhme scheme appears to circle around a tercet pattern, as if the poem were striving towards *terza rima* but never managing to sustain it. In another aspect there are suggestions of Shakespearian and Spenserian elements – quatrains in *abab*, rhyme words carried forward slightly longer than we expect – and, again, of Petrarchan rhymes, in the three times repeated rhyme on 'appear' which runs through the sestet. The rhymes form too a small part of the difficulty presented in lines six to eight, as a result of the rhyme-sequence constituted by lines four to seven – *bacd* – which refuses to resolve or clarify the pattern of rhyme in the poem by offering four successive unrhyming lines.

The formal and syntactic difficulty of these lines is supplanted in line nine by a return to the clear and natural syntax of the sonnet's opening, which, marked off grammatically by a semi-colon and itself terminating emphatically in a colon, ushers in the poem's famous version of an already very famous and immemorial *topos*:

> And on the pedestal these words appear:
> My name is Ozymandias, King of Kings,
> Look on my Works ye Mighty, and despair!

The simplicity of such straightforward, unironic confidence in the tone of the pronouncement, picked up from the poem's rendering of the traveller's style, produces a superbly grand irony. For the simple fact of the matter proposed by the legend on the pedestal is transmuted now into an equally blinding obviousness, but an obviousness in the service of an opposite simple truth. The capitalisations, with their shading of substantives towards the semantic range of personified abstraction, serve to generalise and universalise the moral on behalf of tyranny, and thus are caught in the general inversion effected by the irony. 'Kings', and the 'Works' of the 'Mighty', are always with us, always offer themselves as transcendent in their value, and, as we now see, always end up mocked in time by the vain grandeur of their self-images. The effect of these capitals is recalled in the 'collosal Wreck' of line thirteen, with its implication that the ruin of Ozymandias has a generic kind of significance, a significance that is deeply typical of a whole category of human experience and behaviour. The legend is emphasised in its grand irony by the beautiful weighting of the rhythm in the first half of line twelve – 'Nothing beside remains' – which deploys an initially trochaic movement only to settle to a gravely composed pause on the reasserted iambic pulse of 'beside remains'. 'Remains' is also allowed just a hint of ambivalence – substantive or verb? – which, although fleeting, does serve to imbue the description with a distinct feel of the utterly desolate and deserted remains of the Tyrant's monument.

The closing lines lengthen out an effect of description now quietened to awe-struck contemplation by the momentous clarity of the observed scene's meaning. There is something chilling in the indifferent emptiness of the desert, which has so effortlessly outwaited the tyrant's monument. The epithet 'colossal' reads in this context almost as a jeer; what has finally emerged on a colossal scale is the deluded vanity of thwarted human ambition. The sands are represented in a repeated alliterative pattern which images the conquering endlessness and sameness of the desert; 'boundless and bare', 'lone and level'. The last lines are beautifully composed in their movement, with the very strong pause after 'Wreck' creating a penultimate line of emphatically balanced halves which is then played off against by the steady evenness of stresses in the last line. The poem ends in a calm which marks the arrival at a certainty; there is even a kind of sadness in the tone. The pretentions even of an abominable tyrant can seem, when reduced this completely to ruin, in the end just an instance of a larger vanity of human wishes, with effects which must touch everybody.

But 'Ozymandias' is an elusive poem. Its very certainties are deceptive, its ironies too active to sit comfortably with the ostensible closure of the final lines. Local effects of syntax and diction help to create a semantic texture which is threaded by resonating ironies and ambivalence. These constantly enter implicit questions concerning the apparent drift of the overt ironies. The word 'mocked' in line eight is an obvious example, with its very noticeable pun on 'copied' and 'derided'. The implication is that there has been a conscious awareness by the original artist of the ironies likely to emerge in time from his representation of the tyrant. The mocking is not simply of the subject's actual appearance, though that is certainly one possible sense (the wrinkled lip and sneer of cold command are represented more truly – perhaps bearing in their representation a hint of caricatured exaggeration – than was intended by the commission). But a further possibility for mockery, in the sense of derision, lies in the pretension to permanence in the commissioning of such a monument, with such an inscription. The artist has mocked this project by memorialising, not the personality and regime of the tyrant, but rather his own skill and insight as an artist. However, this achievement then becomes a further victim of the poem's irony, for the sculpture is now ruined and deserted, and appears only to have found a modern audience almost by chance. It has, so to speak, been corrupted as a 'text' in the processes of its transmission through time. It might benefit from the attentions of an editor. The sonnet thus once again returns us to its power repeatedly to disclose previously unrealised perspectives of self-reference and self-critique in its handling of a *topos*; for the sonnet exists in time, just like the sculpture of the tyrant (and, for that matter, just like the traveller, and also the poet who tells us what the traveller said). Has the meaning of the sonnet been taken up and transformed by the ironies of time? Has the skill and insight of its maker, indeed, emerged as the poem's most lasting quality, as against the permanence of the ironic 'moral' it so directly offers?

These questions receive a further twist from other ambivalent elements of diction and phrasing. The syntax of the poem momentarily offers the possibility – as we have already noted – that the 'wrinkled lip' and 'sneer of cold command' have in fact outlasted time and the desert; line seven tells us that they 'yet survive'. But then, in simple fact, they *do* survive, for they are still visible and recognisable on the statue. And, of course, the irony of the poem depends in an obvious way on the continuing existence, in the contemporary world of the sonnet's making, of tyrants like Ozymandias. His ruin holds a lesson for modern tyrants, certainly; but for the lesson to have any point we have also to assume that tyrants continue to exist, to need to have this lesson taught them. We also catch something of the brute reality of the tyrant's earthly power in the 'stamped' of line seven: 'Which yet survive, stamped on these lifeless things'. It is as if the heartless and cruel exercise of power manages to haunt the ruins still, or at least to haunt the traveller's description of the ruins.

These qualities of the rhetoric of 'Ozymandias' lead us, then, in what one critic has called a 'chinese box'-like unnesting of stylistic and thematic terms of reference,[4] beyond an initial meditation on the changes wrought by time on pretensions to power, and towards the realisation of an irony which bears on the poem itself. Is the ultimate effect of this rhetoric to undermine the force of the poem's ostensible moral, by proposing the work of the artist as the only human activity which can defeat time (because the art has proved more durable than the morality)? Or is the sonnet rather itself subject, in the end, to the same ironic strictures which are made to bear on Ozymandias and his monument? For it may be that the sonnet has become, with the passage of time, simply a monument to the vain aspirations of artists. The poem, like Ozymandias' statue, has to maintain some form of material existence in the world; and, this being so, time will corrupt it in the end, and thereby bring into being a destructive irony identical with the one that has transformed the meaning of the legend quoted in the sonnet. The sonnet's deployment of speech marks is suggestive in this respect. The whole of the traveller's story is enclosed by speech marks, but not the legend on the pedestal. This presentation allows the legend on the pedestal to propose itself as a legend for the sonnet also; the poem then in a way anticipates the time when it too will have been left standing, ravaged by time, and lying to be found by some unimaginable audience in a context changed out of all recognition from the one in which it came to exist. The issue that the poem leads us back to is thus ultimately disclosed as that of the mode of existence of the verbal work of art. 'Ozymandias', the poem, offers an instance, cognate with that offered by the ruined statue we read of in

4 Jean Hall, *The Transforming Image: A Study of Shelley's Major Poetry* (London, 1980), p. 21.

the poem, of a human activity which is genuinely able to transcend time, to outlast the conditions and occasions of its making, and in living beyond them to establish the higher kind of existence enjoyed by art as against life.

But this begs a crucial question: *do* verbal works of art exist in a mode which is not subject to the depradations of time? If, as we have already observed, even a poem must have some means of material transmission through time, then a poem must become corrupted, that is, the physical form in which it exists must alter and degrade. It is a question at the heart of the central Romantic lyrics, those Romantic poems which elaborate a critique of their own relation to actuality, and time, and the materials of which they are made (where 'materials' denotes both human character and action in space and time, and language – language-in-print – as the physical medium of the art form). One implicit assumption, for instance, of the 'Ode on a Grecian Urn' is that the Ode, unlike the Urn, cannot be broken by being dropped (or whatever). In this sense the poem can be thought of as exempt from the limits discovered in the kind of existence known to the Urn, which inhabits a realm that is in many ways rather chillingly less as well as more than human. Poetry, in common with the other forms but in distinction from the plastic arts, exists in time as well as space. With each new reading the Ode *has* to be experienced in time. The 'Ode on a Grecian Urn' unfolds in a linear way – unfolds along the syntagmatic or horizontal axis, as it were – as well as existing in a set of fixed structural relations between its constituent parts which exist spatially, like a painting. More tellingly, the verbal material of the art can easily be thought of as fundamentally non-physical – a poem can exist in its entirety in a single person's memory, for instance, and enjoy that mode of transmission for, possibly, a long time – so that there is a temptation to think of literary artefacts, or at least shortish ones, as not depending on the realisation of a finite given physical form subject to the ordinary canons of decay.

And yet in an important sense the Ode *has* been, as it were, 'damaged'; for example by the textual crux affecting the punctuation of the last two lines (which of course has an important bearing on any consistent reading of the Ode's argument).[5] So that the Ode does not after all escape the conditions of existence of those fleetingly physical

5   The known facts in the transmission history of the 'Ode on a Grecian Urn' are set out in Jack Stillinger, *The Texts of Keats's Poems* (Cambridge, Massachusetts, 1974), p. 70; see also Robert Gittings, *The Odes of Keats and Their Earliest*

mortals (the ones who know 'all breathing human passion', unlike the
ones depicted on the Urn) whose experience is at once reduced and
idealized, immortalised and frozen in the representation. 'Ozymandias'
offers no textual crux so obviously striking as the famous problem at
the end of Keats's Ode; but the record of the sonnet's transmission
through time, from the Christmas of 1817 when it came into existence, up to the present day, does in fact throw up enough variation in
the forms taken by the poem to pose a similar problem. Is the poem
somehow to be thought of as exempt from the conditions of material
decay which determine the fate of Ozymandias and his statue? If the
poem can be so thought of, then such a conception can only be
supported by an idealist view of the mode of existence of literary
artefacts, which in its turn generates serious difficulties. But the issues
require first a survey of those changes in form which the poem can be
shown to have undergone.

'Ozymandias' was first published in Leigh Hunt's *Examiner* of 11
January 1818, over the name GLIRASTES.[6] It had probably been composed between 26 and 28 December 1817, in friendly competition
with Horace Smith, who stayed with the Shelleys at Marlow on those
dates, and whose own poem on a closely similar subject was also
published in the *Examiner*, on 1 February 1818.[7] Hunt was probably
also himself involved in, or at least present at the competition, as he
later mistakenly sent Shelley's 'Ozymandias' to Keats's editor Richard
Monckton Milnes as the sonnet 'To the Nile' which Shelley is certainly known to have written in competition with Keats and Hunt in
February 1818.[8] Hunt's mistake here strongly suggests that he recalled

Known Manuscripts (London, 1970), p. 70, and Miriam Allott (ed.), *The Poems
of John Keats* (London, 1970), pp. 537–8.
6   The name 'GLIRASTES' appears to be a private domestic joke in the manner
of the 'Grecian' days at Marlowe in the summer of 1817: the word means
something like 'Dormouse-lover' in a playful transliterated Greek coinage;
'The Dormouse' was one of Shelley's nicknames for Mary (see G M Matthews
and Kelvin Everest (eds.), *The Poems of Shelley*, volume 1 (London, 1989), p.
446.
7   For the dates of Smith's visit see Paula R. Feldman and Diana Scott-Kilvert
(eds.), *The Journals of Mary Shelley*, 2 volumes (Oxford, 1987), i, p. 188.
Horace Smith's sonnet appeared in the *Examiner* (No. 527, p. 73) entitled
'Ozymandias'. It was subsequently reprinted in his *Amarynthus the Nympholept*
(1821) under the title 'On a Stupendous Leg of Granite, Discovered Standing
by itself in the deserts of Egypt, with the inscription inserted below'.
8   See Hyder Edward Rollins, *The Keats Circle*, 2 volumes (Cambridge, Massachusetts, 1965), ii, p. 182.

'Ozymandias' too as the product of a competition. Such competitions
would have been under timed conditions, on an agreed specific subject
presumably thrown up by conversation on recent reading or current
affairs.

Shelley's 'Ozymandias' read as follows in its first printed form, in
the *Examiner*:[9]

> I met a Traveller from an antique land,
> Who said, 'Two vast and trunkless legs of stone
> Stand in the desert. Near them, on the sand,
> Half sunk, a shattered visage lies, whose frown,
> And wrinkled lip, and sneer of cold command,
> Tell that its sculptor well those passions read,
> Which yet survive, stamped on these lifeless things,
> The hand that mocked them, and the heart that fed:
> And on the pedestal these words appear:
> 'My name is OZYMANDIAS, King of Kings.'
> Look on my works ye Mighty, and despair!
> No thing beside remains. Round the decay
> Of that Colossal Wreck, boundless and bare,
> The lone and level sands stretch far away.

It is apparent at once that the poem in this form has been carelessly
printed. The speech marks opened in the second line are never closed,
and of the two lines giving the words on the pedestal only the first is
enclosed in speech marks. The full stop after *Kings* seems a little odd,
and fits with a more general impression of heavy punctuation in an
abundance not typical of such a short poem by Shelley. The text
appears to have been complicated in its accidentals in a way conso-
nant with Hunt's practice with his own poetry; plentiful capitalisation,
and particularly the visually mannered 'OZYMANDIAS', reinforce the
impression that Hunt as editor has tampered with the press copy
supplied by Shelley.

The poem's next appearance was in the *Rosalind and Helen* volume
of 1819, where it is included as one of the 'few scattered poems I left in
England' mentioned by Shelley in his 'Advertisement' as having been
selected for the book by 'my bookseller'.[10] The *Rosalind and Helen* text

---

[9] *Examiner* No. 524, 11 January 1818, p. 24 (reprinted unchanged in the
same Number, 12 January, same page).
[10] Thomas Hutchinson (ed.), *The Poetical Works of Shelley* (Oxford, 1904;
revised G. M. Matthews, 1970) 167 ('Ozymandias' is printed on p. 92 of

of 'Ozymandias' was presumably prepared for the press in Shelley's absence in Italy by Peacock, and very probably derives from the *Examiner* text. Its variants are therefore not Shelley's; but it is nevertheless palpably superior to Hunt's version:

> I met a traveller from an antique land
> Who said: Two vast and trunkless less of stone
> Stand in the desert. Near them, on the sand,
> Half sunk, a shattered visage lies, whose frown,
> And wrinkled lip, and sneer of cold command,
> Tell that its sculptor well those passions read
> Which yet survive, stamped on these lifeless things,
> The hand which mocked them and the heart that fed:
> And on the pedestal these words appear:
> 'My name is Ozymandias, king of kings:
> Look on my works, ye Mighty, and despair!'
> Nothing beside remains. Round the decay
> Of that colossal wreck, boundless and bare
> The lone and level sands stretch far away.

The punctuation has here been significantly lightened and rationalised – the speech marks now make sense – and the capitalisation has been cut down. There is one substantive change, in line twelve, where the *Examiner*'s 'No thing' has become 'Nothing'. The semantic effect of this is slight, only moderating the effect of grim definiteness conveyed in Hunt's version; but the prosodic difference is quite marked, because the sequence from trochaic to iambic feet is not present at all in the *Examiner* form. But the *Rosalind and Helen* version is different from the version quoted at the beginning of this essay in one or two minor ways which do nevertheless make a difference at the level of close reading attempted so far. There are for example no suspension points after 'desart', while there now *is* a comma after 'sunk' in the following line. The spelling of 'desart' is also different; giving the word in its more archaic form, with the 'a', reacts a little with 'antique' from the previous line to sustain a slightly antiquarian feel in the diction (two adjacent effects in the diction are, of course, much more than twice the weight of each single one). This introduces perhaps – for the modern reader, whose reception of the spelling 'desart' is now quite different from any possible intention on Shelley's part – a sort of

Shelley's collection *Rosalind and Helen, A Modern Eclogue; with Other Poems* (London, 1819)).

characterising of the traveller, and perceptibly shifts the initial tonal register of his account, nudging it towards a fanciful, yarn-enhanced idiom which is less reliable than the 'archaeologist' mode noted above.

The two early printed forms of Shelley's sonnet, in the *Examiner* and in the *Rosalind and Helen* volume, provided the bases for all the very many subsequent printed versions which appeared throughout the nineteenth century, and which gave 'Ozymandias' its currency and popularity. Most anthologies drew their texts of the sonnet from one or other of the major Victorian editions of Shelley's poetry, usually either Mary Shelley's 1839 edition, or one of the Buxton Forman editions; these in their turn had based their texts on the *Rosalind and Helen* text quoted above. Why they should have done so seems obvious, but it is nevertheless worth spelling it out. The *Examiner* text is unShelleyan (and at the same time Hunt-like) in its accidentals, and contains palpable error (particularly in the use of speech marks). The *Rosalind and Helen* text is most easily explained in its differences from the *Examiner* version as a thoughtful and careful correction of that version. There is nothing to suggest that the *Rosalind and Helen* text actually benefited from a corrected manuscript supplied by Shelley himself, so that version is in fact further from the source of the poem than the *Examiner*; but it is truer to that source in the sense that it more closely resembles the presentational forms known to have been preferred by Shelley in those poems which he himself saw through the press, or for which he prepared careful copy which survives. The *Rosalind and Helen* version also better serves a consistent and attentive reading (this point does not necessarily follow from the previous one, but in Shelley's case it usually does). The grounds for such a claim, needless to say, can only be the full articulation of just such a reading, and the conviction carried by those grounds can only be, well, simply the persuasive power of the reading. But if it is to be persuasive it must be a careful reading of the text in some fixed and definite form or other. The provenance of the text, as we have seen, throws up a variety of exactly specific forms for the poem, and it follows that there is a kind of legitimacy in claiming that there can now be no authoritative final form for the poem. The process by which the text has survived at all has introduced an indeterminacy at the formal level, in both accidentals and substantives, which can then be called on in support of critical methodologies which wish to claim that there can never be anything authoritative in the claims of a reading. Indeed practitioners of such methodologies would cheerfully reverse the criteria and point to indeterminacy, 'play', as the *point* and proper nature of all critical reading; the heightened consciousness in recent years of the significant element of indeterminacy introduced into any text by the processes of its material transmission thus becomes grist to that critical mill.

But a reading has in practice to settle for one particular form of a text. This must remain true even when the objective of the reading is to bring variant forms into full play in the critical activity; for to be recognised as significant variants they must involve formal differences which are perceptible (i.e. they must be noticeably different from each other), and they will therefore make a difference, when incorporated, to the text as a whole. So that even the most eclectic approach to what constitutes the text of 'Ozymandias' will stay in the business of comparing different distinct versions of the poem; and that will be a pointless activity without an overarching purpose of literary judgement. The fact that the sonnet can take various forms – in mathematical terms, very many, in fact almost limitless forms – is beyond doubt. But this makes no difference to the critical activity in the end, because any reading which seeks to take account of the whole poem must be a reading of the whole poem in one particular form or another, however eclectic the method by which the given form has been arrived at. And that one form, while not necessarily confined in a purist way to some single actual form taken in the course of its transmission through time by the poem, then becomes at once the occasion for critical activity, and also its justification. Variants from it are meaningful because of the difference they make to interpretation if they are substituted in the text under interpretation. Therefore, far from demonstrating the limitless scope for meaning in any text, as realised in the fact of its variant forms, the existence of variant forms demonstrates the relatively closed semantic field of any specific choice of readings within a single version of the text.

The situation produced for criticism by the fact of multiple variants in a text, coupled with the various technical possibilities which now exist for creating new specific forms for the same poem, is not in reality one of a fluid indeterminacy. It is rather that criticism is confronted by a large number of distinct poems, all extremely similar but in fact distinct and autonymous. We can for example easily now envisage a mode of existence for 'Ozymandias' as a series of closely similar poems, each drawing differently on the manuscript and print traditions of the poem, and each thus constituting an object of study for analysis. Any comparative activity between versions will have to assume in advance the prior existence and artistic integrity of each

'Ozymandias', because differing functions of details from version to version must make recourse initially to functions within distinct versions (for example the difference made by retaining or discarding a comma at the end of the first line will depend on the rest of the text as it appears in each case). Literary judgement is then still the only court of appeal for deciding on a best version. And that best version will usually turn out to be the one anyway dictated by the exercise of intellectual responsibility in the handling of the documents recording the transmission history, because the most compelling set of specific decisions about accidentals and substantives has at least a very good chance of being that set produced by the poet's own judgement.

In the context of these reflection we might propose that Shelley's sonnet has in fact not been subjected to the same irony-generating corruption and decay in its form, as the consequence of maintaining existence in time, that the poem finds in the fate of Ozymandias's statue. This introduces yet another dimension of irony, for the poem is in this light in a contrastive relation to the material monument it describes. The record points to change in the text, but the record is fairly complete, and can in combination with a critical intelligence still be made to yield a 'best form' for the poem, one which preserves the best possibility for complex and self-consistent reading. It goes without saying that this 'best form' will be arguable, and will depend for its authority on two assumptions: that sustained consistent reading of poetry is possible; and that some readings make better sense than others.

The case of 'Ozymandias' has recently taken a further turn in its textual history. In the eighteen-nineties the Shelley family presented some of the manuscripts in its possession to the Bodleian Library, including the notebook (now known by its Bodley classification of 'Bodleian MS. Shelley e. 4') which contains rough draft notes for, and a complete version of 'Ozymandias'. Although the notebook has been in the public domain since the nineteenth century, amongst Shelley's major editors only C. D. Locock, and more recently Neville Rogers, have made much use of its material. The 'e. 4' notebook has now appeared in the Garland series of photofacsimile reproductions with transcriptions of all the significant Shelley manuscript material in the Bodleian Library, in a volume expertly edited by Paul Dawson. His transcription of the notebook version of 'Ozymandias' reads as follows:

> I met a traveller from an antique land,
> Who said – 'two vast and trunkless legs of stone

> Stand in the desart . . . near them, on the sand,
> Half sunk a shattered visage lies, whose frown,
> And wrinkled lips, & sneer of cold command,
> Tell that its sculptor well those passions read
> Which yet survive, stamped on these lifeless things,
> The hand that mocked them, & the heart that fed;
> And on the pedestal, this legend clear:
> My name is Ozymandias, King of Kings,
> Look on my Works ye Mighty, & despair!
> No thing remains beside. Round the decay
> Of that colossal Wreck, boundless & bare
> The lone & level sands stretch far away.'–[11]

By Shelley's own standards, this is a very carefully punctuated text. The attention to relatively light punctuation at the end of lines is particularly unusual and strongly suggests that Shelley had given thought to the poem's accidentals, and had consciously decided on the form of punctuation as given here. The critical account offered above in fact makes this assumption in arriving at a text for the sonnet on which to base a reading. Various material features of the notebook fair copy bear out the impression of a meditated final form: the writing is strikingly neat and spaced attentively on the page; an isolated letter 'I' towards the top left-hand corner of the page suggests a false start in transcription by Shelley, presumably because he wished to give the title, formally centred and almost printed in lower case, but at first omitted to do this.

There are on the other hand certain features of this text which do not suggest a final form. In the second line Shelley has crossed out the first word – 'He' – and replaced it with 'Who' written to its left (from the indentation it is clear that this change must have been made after the transcription had been finished). This indicates that Shelley was still making substantive changes to the sonnet after the time of the transcription; it seems in fact reasonable to assume that this transcript was made at the actual time of the sonnet competition with Hunt and Horace Smith. The *verso* side of the same page in the notebook contains some eighteen lines of very rough draft notes, fragments and entire lines for the sonnet, and these presumably represent Shelley's working materials for rapid composition. The drafts are in a state of such chaos that it is plausible to infer that Shelley was also working

---

11   Donald H. Reiman (ed.), *The Bodleian Shelley Manuscripts*, Volume 3, Paul Dawson (ed.), *Bodleian MS. Shelley e. 4* (London, 1987), pp. 340–43.

with a loose sheet, or something similar, where the poem was pulled into a workable shape before the neat and formal transcription on the other side of the notebook page.

The notebook version of 'Ozymandias' differs quite markedly from the first published version of the sonnet which appeared in Hunt's *Examiner*. The system of accidentals is completely different, and it is overwhelmingly likely that this difference is due to editorial interference by Hunt. The accidentals of the notebook version therefore have a very strong claim to authority in any new edition of the poem; they are consistent, and they yield the best possibilities for reading. But while Hunt liked to tinker with the punctuation, spelling, capitalisation, and other features of other writers' presentational forms, he did not lightly take the further and much more drastic step of altering words. And yet the *Examiner* version contains emphatic substantive variations from the notebook version: 'lip' for 'lips' in line five; 'these word appear' for 'this legend clear' in line nine; 'No thing beside remains' for 'No thing remains beside' in line twelve. All of these changes can be understood as alterations prompted by Shelley's aesthetic judgement, and as changes for the better. The 'lips' of the notebook version suggest too strongly actual and so-to-speak congenital physiognomic features, rather than the arrogant deliberately curled 'lip' of a contemptuous sneer. The notebook line, 'And on the pedestal, this legend clear', has an almost clumsy syntactic inversion, and an odd grammatic compression, which suggest unpractised strain in meeting the demands of the form. The differences made rythmically, and also in the range of possible semantic association, by choosing 'beside remains' rather than 'remains beside', have already been discussed in some detail.

The likeliest explanation of these variants is simply that Shelley supplied Hunt with a modified version of his poem for publication in the *Examiner*, and it follows that the substantive text of the *Examiner* version should be regarded as authoritative, There is no difficulty in then combining this substantive text with the system of accidentals employed in the notebook version, to arrive at the text of 'Ozymandias' quoted at the beginning of this essay.[12]

---

[12] There is one anomaly in the text as constituted here; the reading 'Nothing' in line 12 has in fact no sanction in any manuscript or early printed source. But Shelley's corpus reveals only one instance of rendering 'nothing' as 'no thing' where the context allows for real ambiguity, and that is a context ('Hymn to Mercury', stanza 79, line 3) where the metre absolutely demands it.

The documents which bear on this editorial decision do offer between them a very considerable range of variation, in substantives and accidentals, which could be regarded as raw material for potentially infinite specific forms for the poem, concocted at the whim or pleasure of each individual reader of the poem. New computer-based 'hypertext' forms for future editions of Shelley's works, comprising in disc form the whole range of known printed and manuscript forms of each poem, and in a format facilitating the instant creation of new texts incorporating variants eclectically, will make it easy, soon, for each reader to 'make up' his or her own unique text. But this activity will not dissolve the obligation for literary interpretation which attends to the discrete and autonymous life of a specific single version, conceived as a work of art. On the contrary, as this discussion has tried to show, the fact of difference between specific versions actually gives a coherent grounding for questions of literary judgement; the poem in this or that particular form can be shown to work differently, as a poem, given the describable effects of variant readings when substituted one for another. The poem can be understood to exist in a mode which is, to return to our earlier questions, different from the mode of existence of the statue of Ozymandias. But one final irony can then emerge; for Ozymandias's statue in fact exists for us now only within the rhetoric of Shelley's poem, and so it too will after all enjoy a kind of imaginative life; for as long, at least, as Shelley's editors can work, in collaboration with the practices and purposes of his art, to remake his texts in their original image.

Shelley and the Ambivalence of Laughter

TIMOTHY WEBB

With the exception of Byron, the major Romantic poets are not often associated with the comic or with satire. The relative scarcity of such elements in their poetry has tended to encourage simple biographical explanations and to confirm a general assumption that Romantic poets were essentially humourless. Yet in some cases at least, even the biographical evidence might suggest that there is a self-justifying circularity in this argument.

The case of Shelley provides an instructive example. On the surface, it would seem that Shelley's strict sense of moral purpose and the intensity of his political and metaphysical concerns made it difficult for him to laugh. Writing of his early years, Thomas Jefferson Hogg referred to 'the gravity of Shelley and his invincible repugnance to the comic' and recorded how Shelley had once accused him of laughing at everything: 'I am convinced that there can be no entire regeneration of mankind until laughter is put down!' Edward Trelawny, who knew him in the last months of his life, also observed that 'He did not laugh, or even smile, he was always earnest.'[1] From biographers such as these one certainly gets the impression that he was a man more laughed against than laughing.

Yet Shelley's own self-criticism suggests a capacity for irony and self-mockery which immediately exonerates him from the charge of seriousness which he brings against his own lightly disguised poetic persona in *Julian and Maddalo*. He was also acutely aware of the uses of laughter and seems to have distinguished between its several varieties and purposes. This concern and this tendency in Shelley can be detected in his poetry which exhibits an ambivalence towards laughter that has never been fully recognized. What the poetry reveals is not so much an unrelenting earnestness as a suspicion of laughter when it is associated with the human capacity to tyrannize and to rejoice in the violent exercise of power. So in *The Revolt of Islam* the murdering horsemen 'with loud laughter for their tyrant reap / A harvest sown with other hopes' (lines 2393–4) while in *Peter Bell the Third* Peter

---

[1] T. J. Hogg, *The Life of Shelley* (London, 1933), I.88; II.23; *Records of Byron, Shelley and the Author*, ed. David Wright (Harmondsworth, 1973), p. 55.

describes the yeomen who 'laugh with bold triumph till Heaven be rent' (line 649). In *The Revolt of Islam* 'the conquerors laughed / In pride' (lines 2432–3) while in *Prometheus Unbound* the multitude laughs loud as the victims of religious intolerance are 'Impaled in lingering fire' (I.611–2). In *Queen Mab* God is faced with the charge that 'thou didst laugh to hear the mother's shriek' (VI.119) while Count Cenci laughs in his sleep as he invokes a father's curse (IV.3.20). At times this Gothic expressiveness becomes hysterical, if chilling; so in *The Revolt of Islam* Pestilence manifests itself 'With a loud, long, and frantic laugh of glee' (line 2764). Most characteristically, though, laughter seems to be a weapon in the struggle for ascendancy. In *Prometheus Unbound* the Furies taunt Prometheus when they 'laugh into thy lidless eyes' (I.479) and he is influenced by this contagious mockery so that, as he confesses, 'I grow like what I contemplate, / And laugh and stare in loathsome sympathy' (I.450–1). Prometheus tells the Furies that 'I laugh your power, and his who sent you here, / To lowest scorn' (I.473–4) while the Furies soon retaliate with echoic retribution: 'Dost thou faint, mighty Titan? We laugh thee to scorn' (I.541). Evidently, this kind of laughter (which also marks the behaviour of Count Cenci and of the Cyclops) is allied to that vicious circularity of offence and retribution from which Prometheus attempts to disentangle himself.

Yet if laughter is often a danger and a sign of moral corruption, it can also be energizing and positive. Shelley's own poetry clearly shows that he distinguishes between the negative and the positive polarities both in his figuring of laughter and in his own practice as a writer. Though he can be witty (as in *Letter to Maria Gisborne*) or comical (as in *Swellfoot the Tyrant*) he most characteristically exhibits what he himself described as 'the animation of delight'. This animation is often closely associated with a laughter which is positive and life-enhancing. So in *Julian and Maddalo* the 'rather serious' narrator recalls his horseback conversations with Maddalo, 'the swift thought / Winging itself with laughter' (lines 28–9). This momentum, which gently translates the Homeric allusion into the language of comic energy, can be detected not only in human life but in the operations of the universe. The voice of 'The Cloud' laughs 'as I pass in thunder', laughs 'to see the stars whirl and flee', and silently laughs at its own cenotaph. This positive laughter can be contrasted to the hoarse laughter of the thunder in *Prometheus Unbound* (I.715) which is a negative feature of that fallen world from which the lyric drama gradually releases itself. In the final act the Earth rejoices to hear its volcanic fire-crags 'Laugh

with a vast and inextinguishable laughter' (IV.334). Here the later
emphasis corrects and reverses the negatives of the first act where the
laughter is vengeful and self-enclosed; at the same time, the inextinguishable laughter of the Homeric gods is also translated into an
utterance of universal affirmation.[2]

The complexities of Shelley's responses to laughter are brought into
sharp focus by the sonnet 'To Laughter' which was first discovered
among the Scrope Davies papers in Barclay's Bank in Pall Mall as
recently as 1976:

> Thy friends were never mine thou heartless fiend:
> Silence and solitude and calm and storm,
> Hope, before whose veiled shrine all spirits bend
> In worship, and the rainbow vested form
> Of conscience, that within thy hollow heart
> Can find no throne – the love of such great powers
> Which has requited mine in many hours
> Of loneliness, thou ne'er hast felt; depart!
> Thou canst not bear the moon's great eye, thou fearest
> A fair child clothed in smiles – aught that is high
> Or good or beautiful. – Thy voice is dearest
> To those who mock at Truth and Innocency;
> I, now alone, weep without shame to see
> How many broken hearts lie bare to thee.[3]

Early interpretations of this poem have been rather predictably biographical in their emphases. Neville Rogers suggested that Shelley is
deploring the insensitivity of *somebody* who cannot feel 'the love of
such great powers'. He also endorsed a conjecture of Richard Holmes
that 'the "somebody" is likely enough to be Scrope Davies, about
whose brand of fun Byron wrote, after being visited by him in 1811,

---

[2] For an account of Shelley's 'animation of delight', see Timothy Webb,
'Shelley and the Religion of Joy', *SIR*, 15 (1976), 357–82. Plato considered
inextinguishable laughter unworthy of the gods but Proclus interpreted it in
terms of the exuberant operations of the universe (see 377 for Thomas Taylor's
version of the Proclus). For a general account of Romantic attitudes, see Mark
Storey, *Poetry and Humour from Cowper to Clough* (London, 1979).
[3] *The Poems of Shelley*, I, ed. Geoffrey Matthews and Kelvin Everest (London,
1989), p. 520. For the characterization of laughter, compare 'hollow heart / Of
monarchy' (*Hellas*, lines 954–5) and the hypocrites with 'hollow hearts' in *The
Revolt of Islam* (line 3608).

"ours was but a hollow laughter" '.[4] Other commentators have suggested an engagement with Byron himself, though in a manner which
is more cautiously qualified. Timothy Burnett and Judith Chernaik
speculated: 'Conceivably it was Byron, the butt of caricature and
cartoon, whose heart lay bare to laughter'.[5] The theory has also been
floated by Kelvin Everest and Geoffrey Matthews that the poem is an
act of dissociation from Mrs Godwin, whose misrepresentations of the
Shelleys to her stepdaughter Fanny Imlay provoked her to complain
directly to the supposed offenders that she was 'your laughing-stock
and the constant beacon of your satire'.[6] Yet it is important to respect
the integrity of Shelley's poems and to mark its decorous distance from
the overtly personal or historical. Shelley's 'I, now alone' might be a
trace of a personal relationship which remains unparticularized or it
might be a recoil from a kind of laughter which presumes on a false
congeniality or sociability (this interpretation would be much strengthened if we could assume that Shelley's fiend was a slip of the pen for
'friend').[7] In either case, the text suppresses the evidence and addresses
itself 'To Laughter'. It is probable that behind the poem there lies a
series of meetings with Byron, whose own brand of mockery may well
be reflected in the terms applied to laughter itself and who had himself
feelingly described in *Childe Harold* how 'Laughter, vainly loud, / False
to the heart, distorts the hollow cheek, / To leave the flagging spirit
doubly weak'.[8] Yet Shelley's sonnet is not a specific critique but at
most an 'indirect response' which transcends the particularities of the
individual character or the individual occasion in search of a truth
whose application is closer to the universal.

At first sight, this approach may seem not only surprising in its
avoidance of the particular but forbidding, even perhaps disturbing, in
its moralistic rigour; yet it is consistent with those basic distinctions
concerning laughter which have already been outlined and it deserves

---

[4] Neville Rogers, 'The Scrope Davies "Shelley Find" ', *Keats-Shelley Memorial Bulletin*, 28 (1977), 2–3; Richard Holmes, 'Scrope's Last Throw', *Harper's
Magazine* (March 1977), cited in Rogers 2–3.

[5] Judith Chernaik and Timothy Burnett, 'The Byron and Shelley Notebooks
in the Scrope Davies Find', *RES*, n.s. 29 (1978), 41.

[6] *The Poems of Shelley*, pp. 519–20.

[7] A slip in copying might be indicated by the imprecise rhyme between *fiend*
and *bend* but the evidence of Shelley's practice elsewhere seems to be incon-
clusive. Fiendish laughter would be in keeping with the Gothic element in
Shelley's imagination (see, for example, *The Revolt of Islam*, line 4324).

[8] Chernaik and Burnett, 'The Byron and Shelley Notebooks', 41.

close consideration. To begin with, it is clear that Shelley is not proscribing all laughter indiscriminately: the laughter of which he dissaproves is afraid of 'A fair child clothed in smiles', which may perhaps be taken to represent the laughter of innocence, the simple, joyful, guileless and accepting laughter which, for example, we hear throughout Blake's *Songs of Innocence*, most specifically, of course, in the poem called 'Laughing Song'. The nature of the dangerous and undesireable laughter to which Shelley addresses himself emerges most clearly when he says: 'Thy voice is dearest / To those who mock at Truth and Innocency'. This laughter is mocking and cynical; it is opposed to 'aught that is high / Or good or beautiful'; it jeers at everything that is most sacred and perhaps, because most sacred, most vulnerable. It is not a friend to Hope 'before whose veiled shrine all spirits bend / In worship': for Shelley this is a peculiarly crucial dereliction. In his adaptation of the virtues advocated by Christianity, Hope assumed major importance; three years after he composed the sonnet to laughter, he wrote to his friends the Gisbornes: 'Hope, as Coleridge says, is a solemn duty which we owe alike to ourselves & to the world – a worship to the spirit of good within, which requires before it sends that inspiration forth, which impresses its likeness upon all that it creates, devoted & disinterested homage'.[9]

The image of the veiled shrine is not, then, an idle or a random one but expresses Shelley's belief that Hope is a propensity within man himself, a force for good which may properly assume the status of a divinity. In the sonnet, Hope is linked to Conscience, another great power which is unable to find a throne within the hollow heart of laughter; the link is a close one since conscience seems to have borrowed the rainbow-coloured dress which is more traditionally associated with Hope. Like Hope, Conscience is a humane virtue based on a recognition of responsibility; like Hope, it arises from within the individual and, like Hope, it can be destroyed by cynicism. In fact, the sonnet is notable for the compassion it displays towards the victims of mocking laughter: 'I . . . weep without shame to see / How many broken hearts lie bare to thee'. These lines anticipate that moment in *Julian and Maddalo* when, as Julian remembers, both he and Maddalo were overcome by the Maniac's story and 'Wept without shame in his society' (line 516). They also seem to anticipate one of Shelley's most celebrated lyrics, 'When the lamp is shattered', which was written six

9   *The Letters of Percy Bysshe Shelley*, II, ed. F. L. Jones (Oxford, 1964) p. 125.

years later; there, Shelley laments the perversity of Love, who chooses for his nest the frailest of hearts and is left 'naked to laughter / When leaves fall and cold winds come'.[10] The anticipation is certainly of interest in spite of the difference of tone; in particular, a sense of vulnerability is common to both passages. Yet the 'broken hearts' of 'To Laughter' are open to more than one interpretation. Most obviously, they are the hearts of those who are exposed to the merciless attentions of derisive laughter but it is possible that Shelley is thinking of the mockers themselves whose own hearts are open to the divisive and alienating effects of mockery.

This mockery is opposed not only to basic human qualities but to the natural world: 'Silence and solitude and calm and storm'. Cynical laughter is the product of so-called civilization; a sophisticated activity which stands in opposition to the fresh and unspoilt impulses of nature. 'Thou canst not bear the moon's great eye' is Shelley's accusation which suggests not only that mocking laughter is cut off from nature but that it is afraid of exposure, fearful of being laid bare by the moon's unblinking, dispassionate eye. Nature as Shelley presents it here is not obviously attractive, colourful or even energetic; more than anything else, it seems to represent an uncorrupted element in which man can see himself for what he really is. 'Silence and solitude and calm and storm' might remind us that during the summer of 1816 Shelley was persuading Byron to engage with the Wordsworthian example, and that his course of instruction eventually bore fruit in the third Canto of *Childe Harold*; more obviously, this language of sublimity carries undertones of Shelley's experiences in the Swiss and Alpine landscapes which he visited in that summer of inspiration. These words should be read in conjunction with the sonnet which was found with them among the Scrope Davies papers:

> Upon the wandering winds that through the sky
> Still speed or slumber; on the waves of Ocean,
> The forest depths that when the storm is nigh
> Toss their grey pines with an inconstant motion,
> The breath of evening that awakes no sound
> But sends its spirit into all, the hush
> Which, nurse of thought, old midnight pours around
> A world whose pulse then beats not, o'er the gush
> Of dawn, and whate'er else is musical

---

[10] Chernaik and Burnett, 'The Byron and Shelley Notebooks', 41.

My thoughts have swept until they have resigned
– Like lutes enforced by the divinest thrall
Of some sweet lady's voice – that which my mind
(Did not superior grace in others shown
Forbid such pride) would dream were all its own.[11]

Here Shelley's concluding simile offers us an early variation on the image of the poet's mind as Aeolian lute which he would have known well from Coleridge and which he was later to explore with a sharper and more original focus. Similar images and ideas are developed at greater length and with greater subtlety in 'Mont Blanc', which was written in late July, probably at much the same time as the sonnets, and a fair copy of which was also found among the papers of Scrope Davies.[12] In 'Mont Blanc' Shelley also explores the relation between the mind and the external world; there too we find an emphasis on the silence and solitude of the mountain scene – 'the still cave of the witch Poesy' bears an obvious relation to the hush which is the 'nurse of thought' (which in turn may owe a debt to 'Tintern Abbey'). Above all, it is the clear, refreshing calm of the landscape which allows Shelley to explore the meaning of the mountain and to acknowledge its power and beauty while divesting it of those false notions of divinity which have crippled mankind and produced 'large codes of fraud and woe' (i.e. unjust systems of religion and politics). Meditating on the power of the human mind in the stillness of the mountain setting, Shelley concludes teasingly:

And what were thou, and earth, and stars, and sea,
If to the human mind's imaginings
Silence and solitude were vacancy?

Thus, silence and solitude are central to Shelley's metaphysical inquisitions and those inquisitions are closely linked to religion, politics, the state of society and the sum of human happiness. Laughter ignores these 'great powers', it removes the conditions for fruitful thought; therefore, Shelley feels justified in banishing it from his presence.

This curious but fascinating sonnet is important because it gives voice to ideas which Shelley continued to develop and which help to

---

11 *The Poems of Shelley*, p. 521.
12 For 'Mont Blanc', see Chernaik and Burnett, 'The Byron and Shelley Notebooks', 45–9.

explain both his own practice as a poet and his attitude to various literary genres. Take for example his views on Restoration comedy. In A *Defence of Poetry* he discusses the history of European drama and its intimate connection with the moral well-being of society. The greatest drama, such as the Greek tragedies, has a moral effect on the audience: 'The imagination is enlarged by a sympathy with pains and passions so mighty, that they distend in their conception the capacity of that by which they are conceived; the good affections are strengthened by pity, indignation, terror and sorrow; and an exalted calm is prolonged from the satiety of this high exercise of them into the tumult of familiar life . . .' This bears an obvious relation to Aristotle's theory of *katharsis* or purgation and concentrates on the positive elements in the experience. Shelley goes on to define the effect of tragedy in terms of what it does not as well as what it does involve: 'In a drama of the highest order there is little food for censure or hatred; it teaches rather self-knowledge and self-respect'.[13] Little room for censure or hatred (that is, mocking laughter); instead, it teaches self-knowledge and self-respect (virtues which, like the conscience and hope of the sonnet, are based on a respect for human potentiality and a willed preference for the progressive). In A *Defence* Shelley then proceeds to examine more closely the connection between drama and the moral temperature of the body politic and, in contrast to the perfection of Greek tragedy, he chooses as an example of what he calls 'the grossest degradation of our drama', the theatre of the Restoration. His analysis ignores specific instances and concentrates on a general account of generic deficiencies:

> Comedy loses its ideal universality; wit succeeds to humour; we laugh from self-complacency and triumph instead of pleasure; malignity, sarcasm and contempt, succeed to sympathetic merriment; we hardly laugh, but we smile. Obscenity, which is ever blasphemy against the divine beauty in life, becomes, from the very veil which it assumes, more active if less disgusting . . .[14]

This formulation certainly looks back to the sonnet 'To Laughter' but it develops and expands Shelley's early ideas as one might expect from an essay which was written five years later and with greater

---

[13] A *Defence of Poetry* in *Shelley's Poetry and Prose*, ed. Donald H. Reiman and Sharon B. Powers (London, 1977), pp. 490–1.
[14] Ibid., p. 491.

discursive latitude. It manifests the characteristic Shelleyan distaste for obscenity (which he could bring himself to condone in a Greek-satyr play like *The Cyclops* or in Goethe's *Faust* but with which he was essentially uncomfortable).[15] It also exhibits a distrust of wit which is often taken to be characteristic of the Romantic poets in general, perhaps because of its apparent substitution of verbal dexteriity for deep human feeling, perhaps because it is based, to use a phrase from Henri Bergson, on a momentary anaesthesia of the heart.[16] Yet even this assumption is not sufficiently precise in the case of Shelley and does not allow for the antitheses of his own reactions. The implications of his resistance become clearer in an anecdote told by Thomas Love Peacock, whose own wit Shelley did admire.[17] Peacock records Shelley's reaction to a passage in Beaumont and Fletcher which he interpreted as making fun of a poor woman and a maid servant. The old woman who is 'grown to marble, / Dried in this brick-kiln' has become 'The true proportion of an old smoked Sibyl' while the maid 'has a husk about her like a chestnut, / With laziness, and living under the line here'. Shelley's reaction was blunt:

> He said, 'there is comedy in its perfection. Society grinds poor wretches into the dust of abject poverty, till they are scarcely recognizable as human beings; and then, instead of being treated as what they really are, subjects of the deepest pity, they are brought forward as grotesque monstrosities to be laughed at.' I said, 'You must admit the fineness of the expression.' 'It is true', he answered; 'but the finer it is the worse it is, with such a perversion of sentiment.'[18]

Shelley, it would seem, resisted that kind of verbal extravagance where the energy was exclusively verbal and appeared to exist at the expense of human compassion. Although he acknowledged the irreducible power of verbal associations in the *Defence of Poetry*, he was never

---

[15] In both cases Shelley translated passages which his editors were not prepared to print. For a discussion, see Timothy Webb, *The Violet in the Crucible: Shelley and Translation* (Oxford, 1976).

[16] Henri Bergson, *Laughter: An Essay on the Meaning of the Comic*, trans. C. Brereton and F. Rothwell (London, 1911), p. 5.

[17] See: 'his fine wit / Makes such a wound, the knife is lost in it' (*Letter to Maria Gisborne*, lines 240–1).

[18] 'Memoirs of Percy Bysshe Shelley' in *The Works of Thomas Love Peacock*, VIII, ed. H. F. B. Brett-Smith and C. E. Jones (London, 1934), pp. 82–3.

susceptible to certain kinds of wit. Poetics are not to be divorced from politics and aesthetics remain subordinate to morality.

Perhaps the most important statement in Shelley's account of comedy is this: 'we laugh from self-complacency and triumph instead of pleasure'. Here he seems to be allowing the possibility of a laughter which is innocent and pleasurable; indeed, when he says 'we hardly laugh, but we smile' we realize that he is reversing the requirements of such purists as Lord Chesterfield, who preferred only to smile, and acknowledging the importance of happy, innocent laughter.[19] But this laughter must not be produced at the expense of others' misfortune; anaesthesia of the heart must not be substituted for sympathetic merriment. This applies not only to the 'poor wretches' of Beaumont and Fletcher but also to those in more affluent circumstances, the denizens of the world of fashion who populate the plays of Congreve, Wycherley, Farquhar and their contemporaries. These plays teach us to mock the deepest feelings of the human heart and they encourage self-complacency rather than the self-knowledge and self-respect inculcated by the Greek tragedians.

When Shelley uses the word *triumph* he is in accordance with the famous definition of laughter given by Hobbes: 'The Passion of Laughter is nothing else but sudden Glory arising from some sudden Conception of some Eminency in our selves, by Comparison with the Infirmity of others, or with our own formerly . . .'. This definition was frequently quoted, discussed and analyzed by the philosophers and essayists of the eighteenth century: for example, Addison writing in the *Spectator* in 1711 expounded Hobbes's theory and spoke of 'that secret Elation and Pride of Heart, which is generally call'd Laughter'.[20] Shelley feared that this sudden glory, this temporary feeling of elation and superiority, was based on a disregard for the better feelings. The yeomen who 'laugh with bold triumph' in *The Mask of Anarchy* embody precisely that alliance between negative laughter and power which is at the centre of his critique. To put it another way, mocking laughter annihilates the efforts of the imagination. The imagination, working through its main agent poetry, is in opposition to the principle of self and enables us to identify sympathetically; ultimately, it

---

[19] 'Observe it, the vulgar often laugh, but never smile, whereas well-bred people often smile, and seldom or never laugh!' *The Letters of Philip Dormer Stanhope Fourth Earl of Chesterfield*, VI, ed. Bonamy Dobreé (London, 1932), p. 2692.

[20] Essay of 24 April 1711, citing Hobbes, *Human Nature*, IX.13.

can help us to rebuild the broken world a little closer to the heart's desire. Comedy and laughter in the negative sense work against this; they shut us up in the narrow rooms of our self-complacency, they encourage us to laugh at the misfortunes of others, they acquiesce in the *status quo*. As Shelley put it: 'At such periods [as the Restoration] the calculating principle pervades all the forms of dramatic exhibition, and poetry ceases to be expressed upon them'.[21]

So Shelley's disapproval of mocking laughter extends to certain varieties of comedy; to satisfy Shelley's exacting taste and principles, comedy need not be banished altogether but it should be alchemized, transformed as in *King Lear* into something 'universal, ideal, and sublime'. Here he is partly in agreement with Hazlitt, who saw in Lear and the Fool 'the sublimest instance I know of passion and wit united' although he professed a general distrust of wit and humour because, unlike serious and impassioned poetry, they did not appeal to 'our strength, our magnanimity, our virtue, and humanity'.[22] And what then of satire, the most obvious generic centre of mockery? A preliminary answer is provided by 'Fragment of a Satire on Satire', a fascinating but rarely cited draft which expresses Shelley's views at some length.[23] This poem seems to have been written in 1820 in response to a vituperative review in the *Quarterly* which Shelley attributed to Robert Southey, although we now know that it was written by J. T. Coleridge. Shelley's reaction to the very personal abuse delivered by Southey/Coleridge was to question the validity of satire which is based on personal animus. This is to put it in rather generalized terms; in fact, Shelley was debating with himself whether he should reply to the review by writing a satire on the reviewer.

The fragment begins with an evocation (or invocation?) of the pains of Hell which is vivid and melodramatic and whose terms of reference suggest the persecutions not of a supernatural realm but of modern Europe:

> If gibbets, axes, confiscations, chains,
> And racks of subtle torture, if the pains

---

[21] *A Defence of Poetry*, p. 491.
[22] *The Complete Works of William Hazlitt*, VI, ed. P. P. Howe (London, 1931), p. 24.
[23] Printed in *The Complete Poetical Works of Percy Bysshe Shelley*, ed. Thomas Hutchinson, rev. by Geoffrey Matthews (London, 1970), pp. 624–5. See: 'As to anonymous calumny it is a much fitter subject for merriment than serious comment' (*Letters*, II.134).

Of shame, of fiery Hell's tempestuous wave,
Seen through the caverns of the shadowy grave,
Hurling the damned into the murky air
While the meek blest sit smiling; if Despair
And Hate, the rapid bloodhounds with which Terror
Hunts through the world the homeless steps of Error,
Are the true secrets of the commonweal
To make men wise and just; . . .
And not the sophisms of revenge and fear,
Bloodier than is revenge . . .
Then send the priests to every hearth and home
To preach of burning wrath which is to come . . .

But of course such measures do *not* make men wise and just and they
are the sophisms of revenge and fear. Behind these lines there lies the
complicated history of Shelley's attitudes to Christianity and his disapproval of the way in which it substituted a bullying system of bribes
and punishments, based on the desire for heaven and the fear of hell,
for a more disinterested, less corruptible virtue. In particular, Shelley
was bitterly opposed to any notion of divinity which made room for
the creation of hell, a place which seemed to bear a distinct similarity
to the prisons and dungeons maintained by human tyrants throughout
the world. 'Hurling the damned into the murky air / While the meek
blest sit smiling' has a downrightness which, in its contrast between
the vivid energies of theological damnation and the self-satisfied inac-
tion of beatitude, the modern reader should recognize as characteristically Shelleyan. The passage seems to exemplify the contrast
which Shelley had drawn in a letter to Peacock on the subject of
Michelangelo's *Day of Judgement*, in which he remarks that Michelangelo is unable to convey the state of beatitude, the glorified bodies
of the Elect being represented as 'very ordinary people' while 'Every
step towards Hell approximates to the region of the artist's exclusive
power'.[24] The meek blest sit smiling, having inherited not only the
earth but a comfortable place in heaven from which they can triumph
over the energetic discomfiture of the damned. Shelley's point here is
that such lurid fantasies are the projections of the darker forces within
ourselves; they implicate those who attempt to project them as much
as those at whom they are directed. They are born of despair and hate,
revenge and fear; they are based on what is worst in human nature.

[24] *Letters*, II.80–1.

In his fragmentary poem, Shelley is talking here not of theology but of satire, yet the imagery suggests an analogy between the motivation of those who propagate the vindictive notion of hell and those who enjoy the vengeful pleasures of satire. Equally, they are trapped in a vicious circle, a self-perpetuating cycle of violence. 'While the meek blest sit smiling' is spendidly poised between the world of literature and the world of theology; we might remember Shelley's description of how we react to Restoration comedy – 'we laugh from self-complacency and triumph, instead of pleasure . . . we hardly laugh, but we smile'. The meek blest enact a role parallel to that of the man of wit; happy in their own triumph, smugly superior to the sufferings of poor wretches. Whatever the satirist may pretend, he presides over a system of rewards and punishments which is self-seeking and vindictive and which therefore fails to make men wise and just. Satire provides a savage pleasure but it has no social or moral value:

> If Satire's scourge could wake the slumbering hounds
> Of Conscience, or erase with deeper wounds
> The leprous scars of callous infamy –
> If it could make the present not to be,
> Or charm the dark past never to have been,
> Or turn regret to hope; who that has seen
> What Southey is and was, would not exclaim,
> 'Lash on!' and be the keen verse dipped in flame . . .

Satire can do none of these things; it cannot arouse the conscience of the offending author nor can it reverse the harm he has done (the scars of infamy do not heal easily). Satire in the realm of literature is the equivalent of revenge in the moral world: both are born of a desire to hit back, to secure an eye for an eye, and both are ineffectual and devoid of social value. Because of his fundamental respect for his fellow human beings and his commitment to the principle of hope, Shelley believed that vindictive satire was undesireable: it could not change the past and it did not look to the future. In the case of Southey, he suggests another remedy, beginning in tones of studied mildness:

> . . . I will only say,
> If any friend would take Southey some day,
> And tell him, in a country walk alone,
> Softening harsh words with friendship's gentle tone,
> How incorrect his public conduct is,
> And what men think of it, 'twere not amiss.

Shelley then modulates into a fiercer tone:

> Far better than to make innocent ink
> With stagnant truisms of trite Satire stink

where the spluttering animus is directed not at Southey but at the spirit of satire. The fragment goes on to invoke in contrast to the stink of satire 'the gentle, fair / And world-surrounding element of air'. Here, once again, mocking laughter and nature are set against each other in Manichaean antithesis as in the sonnet 'To Laughter'.

This disavowal of wounding laughter, this firmly moral (if not even moralistic) rejection of the satirical imperative, might seem to represent some kind of absolute. We must be careful, therefore, to remind ourselves that Shelley never finishes the poem so that it is impossible to be sure what his final position might have been. We should remember too that the obverse of Shelley's benevolence was an anger which has largely been erased from the biographical record but which is clearly attested.[25] The animosity of parts of 'Fragment of a Satire on Satire' itself demonstrates the power of that anger and the potential force of that very satirical propensity which Shelley is there renouncing. Perhaps, then, Shelley's practice is not entirely consistent with his principles and perhaps his affirmation of principle is generated by the felt strength of that anarchic energy which sometimes pulls him away from self-control and self-composure.

In fact, Shelley's poetic career both before and after 'To Laughter' provides examples of the satirical which are readily identifiable. There are passages in *Queen Mab* (for example, Shelley's account of Christ's role in history)[26] which fall into that category, while Shelley's satirical tendency is gratified and given a voice by 'Similes of Two Political Characters of 1819' and other poems of that period. *Swellfoot the Tyrant* was sufficiently pointed to be withdrawn from circulation through the efforts of the Society for the Suppression of Vice yet Mary Shelley, who mentions this fact, also tries to depoliticize the play in her editorial note:

> This drama . . . must not be judged for more than was meant. It is a
> mere plaything of the imagination; which even may not excite

---

[25] The gradual toning down of Shelley's anger can be traced, for example, through the various biographical accounts provided by Leigh Hunt.
[26] See especially *Queen Mab*, VII.84–192.

smiles among many, who will not see wit in those combinations of thought which were full of the ridiculous to the author. But, like everything he wrote, it breathes that deep sympathy for the sorrows of humanity, and indignation against its oppressors, which make it worthy of his name.[27]

Yet, although this may concede too much to those who prefer their Shelley without a cutting edge, it also articulates a case which deserves some consideration. The play's momentum is derived less from the desire to exercise the satirist's prerogative of mocking laughter than from an impulse which is essentially genial and playful. The alliance of indignation and sympathy which Mary Shelley identifies in it also provides a key to the understanding of two major works of Shelley's maturity: *Peter Bell the Third* and *The Mask of Anarchy*.

Both of these poems are Shelleyan variations on the satirical and each makes its own treaty with the satirical impulse. *Peter Bell the Third* is critical of Wordsworth but not without admiration and not without generosity; on the whole, it is written more in sorrow than in anger, and its indignation is good-tempered and based on genuine respect for Wordsworth and his achievements: 'Yet his was individual mind, / And new created all he saw / In a new manner, and refined / Those new creations, and combined / Them, by a master-spirit's law' (lines 303–7). Of course, the poem fluctuates in tone and it includes passages which are bitingly satirical. Yet for the most part these are general in focus and they are aimed more at the social and political context and the corruptions of the city than at the derelictions of Peter Bell, P. Verbovale or William Wordsworth and his friends. The poem is basically generous in spirit and frequently playful but its import is serious enough. Shelley did it less than justice when he referred to it as a 'joke' and 'a trifle unworthy of me seriously to acknowledge' and when he assured Leigh Hunt that he was 'about to publish more serious things this winter'.[28] Whether deliberately, or not, Shelley is minimizing here the serious achievement of his poem; there is much in *Peter Bell the Third* which is amusing, colloquially vigorous and sharply to the point. For example:

> Hell is a city much like London –
> A populous and a smoky city;

---

[27] *Complete Poetical Works*, p. 410.
[28] *Letters*, II.189, 135, 164.

> There are all sorts of people undone,
> And there is little or no fun done;
>   Small justice shown and still less pity . . .
>
> There is a Chancery Court; a King;
>   A manufacturing mob; a set
> Of thieves who by themselves are sent
> Similar thieves to represent:
> An army; and a public debt. (ll. 147–51; 162–6)

The suggestion here of Byron immediately helps to place the poem and to show how Shelley can be witty without betraying his principles. Shelley is cutting enough in his portrayal of the political life of England in 1819; but his driving concern is the condition of the ordinary men and women, and the satirical note is tinged with compassion for their sufferings – 'Small justice shown and still less pity'. In contrast, the Byronic posture is characteristically one which expects little good of human nature; it is humane in so far as it understands only too well the weaknesses of human character and the derelictions of the flesh but only infrequently is it compassionate. Byron manipulates human behaviour, as he manipulates verbal behaviour, for comic effect; his friend Lady Blessington put her finger on this when she said, 'He is the absolute monarch of words and uses them as Bonaparte did lives for conquest without regard to their intrinsic value'. Shelley may be amused by some of the more ridiculous aspects of Wordsworth's behaviour but he is more pained than amused by the older poet's acceptance of a Government post (or a situation in the Devil's employment, as he translates it in *Peter Bell the Third*). Shelley does feel on occasion that politicians and place-seekers are deserving of satire's scourge but the scourge is rarely laid on to gratify his own wounded feelings or to indulge more than fleetingly or indirectly a desire for personal revenge. The essential benevolence of *Peter Bell the Third* is quickly evident if one compares it with Byron's amusing but malicious scourging of Southey and Wordsworth in *A Vision of Judgment* and in *Don Juan*.

Don Juan, in fact, is a suggestive case since, although he found it offensive in places, and although it conflicted with his own principles in more ways than one, Shelley admired it greatly. At times Byron exceeded even the limits which might be conceded to the genre of satire: for example, the Dedication was 'more like a mixture of wormwood & verdigrease than satire'.[29] Yet though he was repelled by such

---

[29] Ibid., 42.

elements and such excesses, Shelley recognized and acclaimed the great virtues of Byron's poetic achievement. In 1820 he told Byron how much he was impressed by many of the passages in the first two Cantos including the love-letter and the account of how it was written – 'a masterpiece of portraiture; of human nature laid with the eternal colours of the feelings of humanity'. With equal candour Shelley went on to qualify this eulogy: 'I cannot say I equally approve of the service to which this letter was appropriated; or that I altogether think the bitter mockery of our common nature, of which this is one of the expressions, quite worthy of your genius. The power and the beauty and the wit, indeed, redeem all this – chiefly because they belie and refute it. Perhaps it is foolish to wish that there had been nothing to redeem'. Several months later he developed this final point in a letter to Marianne Hunt where he discusses the contrast between the im-morality of Byron's behaviour and the general amiability of his nature: 'In Lord Byron all this has an analogy with the general system of his character, & the wit & poetry which surround, hide with their light the darkness of the thing itself. They contradict it even; they prove that the strength & beauty of human nature can survive & conquer all that appears most inconsistent with it'.[30] Shelley had too sensitive a taste for what was genuinely important in literature not to respond to *Don Juan* with its extraordinary poise and poetic energy and its voice 'entirely new and relative to the age'. The moralist who repudiated the wit of Restoration comedy here isolated wit as one of the special virtues of *Don Juan*.

Yet Shelley's response to these virtues is based on his sense of a larger equilibrium: here the terms of his two letters are particularly instructive for they show that what ultimately made the poem accept-able to him was his belief that its truly poetic qualities, its power and beauty and wit, transcended the effect of its darker passages, and its occasional bitter mockery of human nature. And this belief is crucial for an understanding of Shelley's views on the subject of laughter. As we have seen, Shelley's laughter in *Peter Bell* is more generous and less personally vindictive than that of Byron in *Don Juan*; but Byron's laughter can still be accepted so long as its final effect is not to blot out our faith in human nature. Since their first meeting in 1816 Shelley had recognized that Byron was prone to fits of self-contempt which led him sometimes to cynicism and sometimes to despair; although his

---

[30] Ibid., 198, 239–40.

own temperament allowed more oscillations towards the optimistic and although he invested heavily in the future tense, Shelley knew from experience that hope could often appear treacherously similar to despair. What was essential both for the poet and for the reader of poetry, was to learn how to distinguish one from the other. If satire was dedicated to a self-created and self-enclosed vision of hell, then it was no friend of humanity and one could reasonably say to it – *depart*. If on the other hand, it allowed the possibility of hope, rather than the negative laughter of despair, then it might be acceptable and even welcome. In his reading of *Don Juan*, Shelley seems to suggest that it is the stylistic qualities, the vigour and beauty of the linguistic medium itself, which finally release Byron the poet and his readers from the threat of everlasting damnation. Shelley's response is now more flexible than it had been when he was unequivocally rejecting Beaumont and Fletcher.

The hope of redemption here is crucial. Both Byron and Shelley believed that man had fallen and continued to fall but Byron, who was always freighted with the grim certainties of a residual Calvinism, could not allow himself those optimistic intimations which fitfully but recurrently illuminated the darkness of Shelley's anxieties. This is the essential difference between their two versions of the Prometheus story. Byron's is the stoical but melancholy 'Prometheus' and Shelley's is the 'beautiful idealism' of *Prometheus Unbound*. For Shelley hope was a solemn duty which we owe alike to ourselves and to the world. It was a moral commitment as well as a psychological and religious intimation. This commitment may help to explain both the function of the satirical elements in *The Mask of Anarchy* and its moral and narrative structure. Even Shelley's detractors are forced to concede the powerful precision with which he introduces his rogues' gallery of the forces which claim to govern the country while effectively imposing a tyrannous control in their own interests:

> I met Murder on the way –
> He had a mask like Castlereagh;
> Very smooth he looked, yet grim;
> Seven bloodhounds followed him:
>
> All were fat; and well they might
> Be in admirable plight,
> For one by one, and two by two,
> He tossed them human hearts to chew
> Which from his wide cloak he drew.

Next came Fraud, and he had on
Like Eldon, an erminèd gown;
His big tears, for he wept well,
Turned to mill-stones as they fell,

And the little children who
Round his feet played to and fro,
Thinking every tear a gem,
Had their brains knocked out by them.

Clothed with the Bible, as with light,
And the shadows of the night,
Like Sidmouth next, Hypocrisy
On a crocodile rode by.

These lines are harsh, and grotesquely satirical; Shelley would be hard pressed to prove that we cannot hear in them the voice of mocking laughter. But, once again, one notices that the mocking laughter is held in check, softened and qualified by the tone of compassionate concern for the little children (with its pointed Biblical echo). More important still are the ways in which this opening passage is developed and its relation to the structure of the whole poem. Shelley's concern here (as in most of his poetry) is to see how the fallen world can be redeemed, to imagine, if he can, how beautiful an order can spring from the dust and blood of this fierce chaos. In 'A Satire on Satire' he rejects a satire which is purely negative, just as in the sonnet 'To Laughter' he rejects a laughter which is purely cynical: in both cases, the reaction is end-stopped, claustrophobic, it confirms and acquiesces in man's fallen state, it makes no attempt to break the bars of the prison. By accepting the hell which is imposed on him, man can perpetuate it and confirm its reality; by questioning it, he can discover that the apparent hell is only the product of a certain mode of perception and not an inalienable reality of the human condition: 'The mind is its own place, and of itself can make a heaven of hell, a hell of heaven'.[31] So The Mask of Anarchy must attempt to stop the apparently inexorable progress of Murder, Fraud, Hypocrisy and their allies and substitute another movement, must endeavour to find a structure for hope even from so unpromising a beginning. Shelley's problems and the nature of his solution are nicely illuminated by a remark of Carl Woodring in his study of Politics in English Romantic

---

[31] A Defence of Poetry, p. 505, citing Paradise Lost. I.254–5.

Poetry: '[*The Mask*] has seemed much too long to those interested in it only as satire. Political it certainly is, but less satiric than prophetic'.[32] Less satiric than prophetic: Shelley's gift for sharp satirical observation is evident at the beginning of the *Mask of Anarchy* but his principles are not satisfied till that satiric vision has been qualified by a vision of hope. His poem, attempts to do what the poetry of mockery is not able to achieve – to 'make the present not to be' and to 'turn regret to hope'.

[32] Carl Woodring, *Politics in English Romantic Poetry* (Cambridge, Mass., 1970), p. 265.

Peter Bell, Peterloo, and the Politics of Cockney Poetry

RICHARD CRONIN

Shelley described *Peter Bell the Third* as a 'party squib'.[1] Most of those who have written about the poem – still only a modest band – have flinched from this description. But *Peter Bell the Third* was written in the autumn of 1819, after news of the killings at Peterloo had sharpened political antagonisms in Britain to a point at which sober observers entertained fears of bloody insurrection.[2] It may be that the poem is not best honoured by attempts to insulate it from the confused and painful circumstances that were its occasion, and that if, as Mary Shelley insisted, the poem is worth preserving because it has 'so much of *himself* in it', then that 'self' had better be recognised as embroiled in the party politics of the day.[3] This is not to say that *Peter Bell the Third* is at all narrow. Its concerns range from Wordsworth and Coleridge, to London, to paper money, to Peterloo, to the evil of a religion that takes as a central article of its creed the notion of damnation, and to the proper relationship between the sexes. It is hard to disagree with Mary Shelley's verdict that no other poem 'contains more of Shelley's peculiar views', but in *Peter Bell the Third* this loose cluster of opinions is organised by Shelley's pained sense of his own irrelevance to the politics of England in 1819.

Donald Reiman has plausibly suggested that 'the proximate cause' of Shelley's rapid composition of *Peter Bell the Third* was the appear-

---

1   *The Letters of Percy Bysshe Shelley*, ed. F. L. Jones (Oxford, 1964), 2, 135.
2   Byron wrote to Augusta Leigh on 13 October: 'you are on the eve of a revolution'. Southey differed only in his confidence that the attempt would be unsuccessful: 'There may be bloodshed, and I am inclined to think there will before the Radicals are suppressed, but suppressed they will be for the time'. See *The Life and Correspondence of Robert Southey*, ed Rev. C. C. Southey (London, 1860), 4, 360. Coleridge thought revolution unlikely, but added: 'I dare not promise as much for *personal* safety. The struggle may be short, the event certain; yet the mischief in the interim *appalling*.' See his letter to Mariana Starke of 15 October 1819, *Collected Letters of Samuel Taylor Coleridge*, ed. E. L. Griggs, 4 (Oxford, 1959), 963.
3   *Shelley's Poetry and Prose*, ed. D. H. Reiman and S. B. Powers, 322. References to *Peter Bell the Third* are to the text of this edition.

63

ance in the *Quarterly* of reviews of Hunt's *Foliage* and of his own *Laon and Cythna*.[4] The reviews acted as a double provocation. First, they presented Shelley's views on religion, on politics, and on sexual behaviour as positions to which he had been driven in a desperate attempt to justify the profligacy of his own life. Secondly, they represented Shelley as an 'unsparing imitator' of Wordsworth, to whom, the reviewer suggests, it must be matter of 'perpetual sorrow to see the philosophy which comes pure and holy from his pen, degraded and perverted as it undoubtedly is, by the miserable crew of atheists or pantheists, who have just sense enough to abuse its terms, but neither the heart nor principle to comprehend its import, or follow its application'. This was the more galling, because Shelley wrongly believed the review to be the work of Wordsworth's closest literary associate and the man to whom *Peter Bell* was dedicated, Robert Southey. He could only have understood it as a declaration of war by the Lake Poets on the whole of that 'miserable crew of atheists or pantheists', amongst whom they would have numbered, in addition to Leigh Hunt and Shelley, Byron, Thomas Moore, Hazlitt, and, if their names had happened to occur to them, Keats and Reynolds. Hunt acknowledged the outbreak of hostilities in the spring of 1819, when he responded to Wordsworth's *Peter Bell* with the most trenchantly dismissive review he was ever to write of a poem by Wordsworth, and chose to publicise, even before Wordsworth's poem had appeared, Reynolds's smugly impudent parody.[5]

Throughout 1819 political and poetical antagonisms intensified. The political conflict reached its climax on 16 August, when a gathering of some 30,000 people met at St Peter's Field in Manchester to petition for reform and to hear an address by Henry Hunt, and were attacked by the local militia. Eleven were killed, and several hundred injured. The Peterloo massacre acted in the autumn of 1819 to

---

4   The review of *Foliage* appeared in *The Quarterly Review*, 18 (1818), 324–35, and of *The Revolt of Islam* in *The Quarterly Review*, 21 (1819), 324–35. On Shelley's belief that the reviews were the work of Southey, see K. N. Cameron, 'Shelley v. Southey: New Light on an Old Quarrel', *PMLA*, 57 (1942), 489–512. On John Taylor Coleridge's claims to be the true author see *Shelley and His Circle*, 6 (1973), 931–2. Byron shared Shelley's mistaken belief. See *Byron's Letters and Journals*, ed. L. A. Marchand, 6 (Cambridge, Mass., 1976), 83.

5   The review of Reynolds's parody appeared in *The Examiner*, no. 591 (25 April 1819), 270. It was written by Keats, and offers his friend only muted, even somewhat embarrassed praise. The review of *Peter Bell* itself appeared the following week in *The Examiner*, no. 592 (2 May 1819), 282–4.

produce a radical simplification of the British political landscape. As Southey wrote: 'It is no longer a question between Ins and Outs, nor between Whigs and Tories. It is between those who have something to lose, and those who have everything to gain by a dissolution of society'.[6] Keats, who had less to lose than most, shared Southey's analysis however much he differed from him in his sympathies: 'This is no contest between whig and tory – but between right and wrong'.[7]

Peterloo polarised the politics of the nation, and it had precisely the same effect on its poetry. The Whiggish *Edinburgh Review* allowed space for the usual diatribe against Cobbett and the other purveyors of twopenny trash, the 'wicked and contemptible set of public writers' who had so successfully undermined the people's confidence in the Whigs as 'their natural leaders', but it reserved its special scorn for 'those unhappy alarmists who see a civil war in every provincial tumult', and of this group the reviewer singles out 'the Laureate and his tuneful friends'.[8] The Lake Poets were commissioned en bloc into the Manchester yeomanry. Tory journals simply reversed the tactic, associating all poets who had shown themselves sympathetic to reform with Cobbett and Henry Hunt. *Blackwood's* responded to the Manchester killings with a tastelessly jocose little piece based on the assumption that Leigh and Henry Hunt were near relations. 'No-one', we are told, 'can listen for five minutes to the oral eloquence of Henry Hunt without being reminded in the most lively manner of the written wisdom of Leigh', and this is to be expected, for 'the Cockney School of Politics . . . is so intimately connected with the Cockney School of Poetry, that it is almost impossible to describe the one without using many expressions equally applicable to the other'.[9] The poets of England were divided by Peterloo into two ranks, and gazed at each other in mutual defiance. Poetry had been subsumed into politics so fully that when Keats tried to imagine the acclamation that would greet any great work of art, his mind turned instinctively to the crowds he had seen lining the streets of London to cheer Henry Hunt on his return from Manchester.[10]

---

6   *The Life and Correspondence of Robert Southey*, 4, 360.
7   *The Letters of John Keats*, ed. H. E. Rollins (Cambridge, 1958), 2, 180.
8   See the review article entitled 'State of the Country', *Edinburgh Review*, 32 (October, 1819), 293–309.
9   *Blackwood's Edinburgh Magazine*, 5 (September, 1819), 639–42.
10   *The Letters of John Keats*, 2, 180. Keats writes: 'I have no doubt that if I had written Othello I should have been cheered by as good a mob as Hunt'.

Shelley responded to Peterloo with the composition of a group of poems unique in his oeuvre, poems in which Shelley identified himself as fully as he could with the crowds who gathered to hear Henry Hunt, and the still larger number who had found their political education in the numbers of Cobbett's *Political Register*. The power of these poems, of which the masterpiece is *The Mask of Anarchy*, comes from their willingness to subordinate poetry to politics, from Shelley's suppression of his own voice in search of the anonyomous authority of the broadsheet balladeer. Early in 1820 Shelley made a rather forlorn attempt to interest Leigh Hunt in their publication. He envisaged 'a little volume of *popular songs* wholly political and destined to awaken and direct the imagination of the reformers'.[11] His announcement, he predicted, would be received by Hunt with a 'smile', a smile produced, no doubt, by Hunt's estimate of the chances of Shelley ever producing anything popular. *The Mask of Anarchy*, 'Men of England', and *A New National Anthem* are written by a poet who has made a conscious decision to disown his literariness as a necessary condition for repudiating the class of which that literariness was the badge.[12] It was a decision quixotic enough, as Shelley realised, to raise a smile, but it was the outcome of Shelley's principled belief that Peterloo had made one duty paramount, the duty to take sides. In these poems Shelley proclaims himself a member of the Cockney School of Politics, and the poems delight in the bracing simplicities that his membership of the school allows him.

Peter Bell the Third is a parallel response to the same events. It is dedicated to one poet, and directed at another: it embraces literature as wholeheartedly as the other poems reject it, and that is the clue to its distinctive character. *Peter Bell the Third* is a poem in which Shelley writes as a member not of the Cockney School of Politics but of the Cockney School of Poetry. I mean by this not merely to indicate the central place of London life within the poem, nor the confession that the immediate inspiration came from the reviews of Wordsworth's poem and Reynolds's parody in the pages of *The Examiner*. I mean that the poem's central areas of concern represent a digest of the issues that had been preoccupying Leigh Hunt in his public writings for the past

---

11 *The Letters of Percy Bysshe Shelley*, 2, 191.
12 Byron, attacking Hobhouse for having reconciled himself with Cobbett and Henry Hunt, writes: 'Why our classical education alone . . . should teach us to trample on such unredeemed dirt', *Byron's Letters and Journals*, 7, 81.

twelve months. There is no evidence that Hunt, to whom Shelley sent the poem, ever made any effort to secure its publication. He may well have been embarrassed by the thought that if, as Shelley insisted, it was published anonymously, it would have been generally assumed to be not Shelley's work but his own, a mistake that the preface with its ironic descriptions of 'Mr Examiner Hunt' as a 'murderous & smiling villain', and an 'odious thief, liar, scoundrel, coxcomb & monster' might have served only to confirm. In any case, the crucial differences between *Peter Bell the Third* and, say, *The Mask of Anarchy*, are best indicated by the differences between the Cockney Schools of Poetry and of Politics, which as even *Blackwood's* recognised, for all that it found it fun to confuse them, remained quite distinct.

The distinction, as *Blackwood's* recognised, was fundamentally a difference of class. Cockney politicians addressed themselves to 'the street mob', whereas Cockney poets wrote for an audience characterised by *Blackwood's* as 'single gentlemen in lodgings and single ladies we know not where'. The Cockney School of Politics had Cobbett's *Political Register* as its leading journal and by 1819 Henry Hunt had become without dispute its leading active politician. The Cockney School of Poetry had *The Examiner*, and it accepted the political leadership of Sir Francis Burdett. *Blackwood's* shrewdly pointed out that Leigh Hunt could never mention Henry without giving vent to 'some malicious sarcasm against that worthy kinsman of his', whereas gentlemanly radicals were afforded very different treatment: 'He talks at times of the Wolseleys, the Burdetts and the Shellys [sic], in terms which would almost persuade one that he really entertained some feelings of decent reverence for the old phylarchic aristocracies of England . . .'. The events of 1819 forced almost all commentators to recognise that English politics had been transformed, that the central conflict was no longer between parties but between classes. The salient fact was the emergence of what Shelley calls in *A Philosophical View of Reform* 'a fourth class' which no longer accepted that 'its interests were sensibly interwoven with that of those who enjoyed a constitutional presence'.[13] It was this class that Cobbett wrote for – indeed it was a class that his writings had done much to bring into being – but it was a class that *The Examiner* with its metro-

---

[13] Quotations from *A Philosophical View of Reform* are taken from *Shelley's Prose: The Trumpet of a Prophecy*, ed. D. L. Clark (Albuquerque, 1954), 230–61.

politan bias and its insecure class base was in no position to address.[14] Peterloo effected a grand simplification of the political landscape for all those who supported the action of the Manchester magistrates and their militia and for their opponents who looked to Cobbett and Henry Hunt as their champions. But for those who took their political lead from Sir Francis Burdett and from the pages of *The Examiner* those same events caused only confusion. Keats thought of writing something that would give 'a Mite of help to the Liberal side of the Question', but, in the end, he chose to mark the autumn of 1819 by writing a poem that seems pointedly to disclaim political reference, *To Autumn*. He recorded his sense that Peterloo had aroused in him difficult, ambivalent responses quietly, with a dry joke: 'Notwithstand [sic] my aristocratic temper I cannot help being very much pleas'd with the present public proceedings'.[15] Byron was driven by the same events into an extraordinary state of vicious hysteria in which grandiose dreams of returning to England to place himself at the head of a popular army alternated with gruesome fantasies of impaling Henry

---

[14] The telling evidence in support of this contention is offered by the circulation figures. At its high point, in 1812, when the glory of Leigh Hunt's imprisonment for seditious libel of the Prince Regent was fresh, the circulation of *The Examiner* rose to 7,000. Thereafter it steadily declined, until, in 1821, when Hunt severed his connection with the journal, it had fallen to less than 3,000. See *British Literary Magazines: The Romantic Age, 1789–1836*, ed. A. Sutherland (Westport, Connecticut and London, 1983), 51. This fall in circulation coincided with a massive increase in the readership for political journalism. In 1816, the weekly circulation of Cobbett's *Political Register* rose to 60,000, and by 1819 even *The Black Dwarf* achieved a circulation of 12,000. See E. P. Thompson, *The Making of the English Working Classes*, 2nd edn (Harmondsworth, 1980), 740–4.

[15] *The Letters of John Keats*, 2, 180. Vincent Newey, in his measured and persuasive study of Keats's politics, discounts a suggestion by Keach that *To Autumn* subsumes within its celebration of natural abundance a vocabulary – 'conspire', 'clammy cells' – that has its origin in the turbulent politics of 1819. Newey insists that the poem 'celebrates a capacity quite opposite to that of political engagement', and is content to add that this represents in itself, 'a tendentious and ideological act'. See 'Alternate Uproar and sad peace: Keats, Politics, and the Idea of Revolution', *The Yearbook of English Studies*, 19 (1989), 265–89. But the poem's refusal of politics is, I suspect, more consciously pointed than Newey allows. In the autumn of 1819 it would have been hard not to recognize in Keats's reaper, asleep in his 'half-reaped furrow', whose scythe 'Spares the next swathe', an iconographic antithesis to the Manchester Yeomanry who so notoriously failed to spare the massed ranks of the reformers.

Hunt on his sword.[16] Keats quietly, and Byron frenziedly, were re-
sponding to a troubled new awareness that questions of political
principle had become entangled with questions of class. *Peter Bell the
Third* represents the most complete and thoughtful exploration of the
same problem.

An example will help to make clear what I have in mind. Amongst
the chaos of types to be found in London are the professional ladies'
men:

> Things whose trade is, over ladies
>   To lean, and flirt, and stare, and simper,
> Till all that is divine in woman
> Grows cruel, courteous, smooth, inhuman,
>   Crucified 'twixt a smile and whimper.   (192–6)

The point of the stanza is clinched by the bold metaphor of its last
line. It is a metaphor that, had *Peter Bell the Third* been accepted for
publication by Ollier in November, 1819, would have jogged the
memory of its readers. In the spring of that year, several issues of *The
Examiner* had been dominated by news of the Westminster election.
Because the franchise at Westminster was unusually wide, allowing all
freeholders the vote, because of its geographical position at the very
centre of the political life of the nation, and because one of its two
elected members was Sir Francis Burdett, the acknowledged spokesman in Parliament for the radical cause, any election at Westminster
was regarded by reforming journals as having a peculiar authority. But
in 1819, as in the previous year, the radical vote was split, and Sir
Francis was returned to Westminster not with a radical colleague, but
together with an orthodox Whig. In both years Burdett seems to have

16 See, in particular, Byron's letter to Augusta Leigh of 15 October 1819, and
his letter to Hobhouse of 29 March 1820. Most remarkable of all is the letter to
Hobhouse of 22 April 1820, in which Byron argues that had the Manchester
Yeomanry 'cut down *Hunt only* – they would have done their duty – as it was –
they committed *murder* both in what they did – and in what they did *not* do'.
In other words, they were guilty of murder on two counts; for having butchered
the 'poor starving populace', and for having failed to butcher Hunt (*Byron's
Letters and Journals*, 6, 228–9, 7, 62–3, and 7, 80–2). I do not know whether to
be more impressed by the viciousness or by the nonsensicality of this. Byron's
response to Peterloo, passed over in embarrassed silence by too many of his
critics, has been ably discussed by Malcolm Kelsall, *Byron's Politics* (Brighton,
1987), 82–8.

insisted on his right to choose his own running mate. In 1818, his choice had fallen on Douglas Kinnaird, and the result was failure. In the following year, after the suicide of Sir Samuel Romilly,[17] the Whig who in 1818 had been elected to serve for Westminster alongside him, Burdett turned to the same set, in fact, to another member of the dining club to which he and Kinnaird (and, incidentally, Byron) belonged. He proposed to the Westminster electors that John Cam Hobhouse should be elected to serve with him for Westminster. On both occasions Burdett was furiously opposed, in print by Cobbett, who accused Burdett of treating the Borough of Westminster as if it was his own private rotten borough, and in person he was opposed by Henry Hunt, who himself stood against Kinnaird, and persuaded Major Cartwright, the veteran supporter of universal suffrage, to stand against Hobhouse. Neither Hunt nor Cartwright was electable, and it might seem that the only result of their intervention had been to split the radical vote, securing one of the Westminster seats for a Whig. But Hunt and Cobbett achieved their two main objectives. First, they succeeded in challenging Burdett's aristocratic leadership of the Radical movement, and secondly they forced Burdett ever closer to aligning himself with their own radical programme: universal adult suffrage, annual parliaments, and a wholesale attack on the system of government patronage that Cobbett named 'old Corruption'. Throughout the 1819 campaign both Hobhouse and Burdett were forced to adopt more and more defiantly Radical postures in an attempt to appease their more enthusiastic supporters. It was in the course of one such speech that Burdett described the Whigs and Tories as 'two thieves, between whom the Constitution had been crucified'.

It was a mistake. The *Courier* seized on the phrase as proof that the radical cause was tainted by impiety. Burdett mustered a lame defence: he had, he claimed, merely been quoting the eminently respectable historian Ralph. In *The Examiner* Leigh Hunt argued that the metaphor, though strong, even shocking, was disinfected of irreverence by the passionate gravity of Burdett's argument.[18] But Burdett and Hunt

---

[17] Romilly cut his own throat on 2 November 1818, not long after he had been elected as one of the members for Westminster. He was distracted by grief at the death of his wife. The reference to suicide in *Peter Bell the Third*, 176, would certainly have recalled Romilly, for, until Castlereagh killed himself in 1822, Romilly was the most famous suicide of the century.

[18] Burdett's speech is reported in *The Examiner*, no. 582 (21 February 1819), 115. In an editorial (121–2) Hunt records how the *Courier* had expressed its

were quite clearly engaged in a damage limitation exercise. Both knew that there were many constituents at Westminster who might champion reform, but not at the cost of respectability, and who, if asked to choose between their political and their religious principles, would not hesitate to sacrifice the former to the latter. It may be that Hobhouse lost the election because Burdett was incautious in his choice of metaphor. In *Peter Bell the Third*, Shelley repeats the offence. His innovation is to transfer the metaphor from the relationship between the parties to the relationship between the sexes, which enables him to press into a single word the three areas of concern that preoccupy him throughout the poem; politics, religion and sexuality.

Shelley's views on these three matters constituted, of course, the major part of that loose bundle of opinions to which he early attached himself, and which he was never to surrender, and they constituted, too, the core of the philosophical radicalism that he shared with Leigh Hunt. But by 1819 those ideas were under pressure. In Shelley's early poetry, in *Queen Mab* for example, ideas exist within a vacuum. The poem assumes that such ideas can operate upon the social world without themselves being part of it. By 1819 that assumption no longer seemed tenable. Byron was driven by Peterloo to doubt whether he could continue to hold political views that were shared by 'blackguards' such as Cobbett and Henry Hunt. Whatever one thinks of the sentiment, it at least entails a recognition that no political theory can exist independent of the social divisions that it seeks to analyse.[19] The philosopical radicals were united in their insistence on the urgent need for a reform of Britain's representative system. They shared, too, a sceptical humanism that held in horror dogmatic religion, especially the kind of religion that sought to discipline its adherents by vigorously alerting them to the threat of eternal punishment, and they shared a belief that human happiness could be achieved only if sexual

'feelings of unmingled detestation' at this 'monstrous sally of impiety'. Hunt retorts: 'The most religious of men might speak as Sir Francis Burdett did, out of the very intenseness of his grave conviction on both subjects – the subject illustrated and the subject illustrating'. Since Hunt well knew that Burdett was no more religious than Hunt was himself, this defence is best described as shifty.

19 Byron wrote to Hobhouse that 'the whole gang' of reformers, only excepting the gentlemanly radicals such as Hobhouse himself, Burdett and Kinnaird, so disgusted him as to make him 'doubt of the wisdom of any principle or politics which can be embraced by similar ragamuffins' (*Byron's Letters and Journals*, 7, 81.

relationships could be placed on a quite new footing. By 1819 they
were forced to recognise that those who opposed their political views
seized eagerly on any opinions that made it possible to associate the
cause of political reform with impiety and with libertinism, for the
obvious reason that such opinions were likely to weaken the appeal of
the reformers to the respectable artisans and traders who were their
natural and most powerful constituency. That was why, of course, in its
coverage of the 1819 Westminster election *The Times* seized so glee-
fully on Burdett's ill-judged use of the word 'crucified'. It was also why
Hobhouse, who had the misfortune of fighting the election shortly
after the publication, with his own notes appended, of the fourth
canto of *Childe Harold*, was assailed throughout the campaign by the
fact of his association with the notoriously libertine poet. It was a
tactic too good for even the radicals to refuse. In the election of the
previous year Burdett's supporters arranged for a letter to be read from
the hustings – not mentioning that it was ten years old – in which
Cobbett warned his correspondent against associating with Henry
Hunt on the grounds that Hunt rode around the country with another
man's wife.[20] Thomas Moore showed himself alert rather than simply
timid when, early in 1819, he wrote to Hunt suggesting that in the
pages of *The Examiner* he curtail his expression of his views on religion
and marriage.[21] It was advice that Hunt honourably refused to take,
but the *Examiners* of that year show very clearly a new nervousness.

News of Peterloo interrupted a prolonged campaign that had dominated the pages of *The Examiner* throughout the summer of 1819, a
campaign for the defence of Richard Carlile, who had been charged

---

[20] Cobbett falsely claimed that the letter was a forgery, and was sued for libel.
His claim may have been a characteristic example of his effrontery, or he may
simply have forgotten having written the letter. The incident is discussed by
G. Spater, *William Cobbett: The Poor Man's Friend* (Cambridge, 1982), 2,
364–6.

[21] Moore recorded the letter in his diary: 'Wrote to Hunt, and gave him a
little hint to keep his theories upon religion & morality somewhat more to
himself, as they shock and alienate many of his best-intentioned readers', *The
Journal of Thomas Moore*, ed. W. S. Dowden (Newark, 1983), 1, 134. Moore
was not just being prim. The pressures reformers were under can be gauged by
the fact that when Cobbett returned to England in the autumn of 1818,
carrying with him the bones of Tom Paine, he was so disturbed by the outrage
he provoked among the religious that he was driven to the extraordinary claim
that he admired Paine only as an economist and that *The Age of Reason* was a
book entirely unknown to him.

with blasphemy for having re-printed Paine's *Age of Reason*. The charges against Carlisle had been orchestrated by the Society for the Suppression of Vice, a powerful and wealthy pressure group that frequently attracted Hunt's hostile notice in these months. The reasons Hunt attached so much importance to the defence of Carlile are neatly summarised in Shelley's own, unpublished, contribution to the campaign: 'In persecuting Carlile they have used the superstition of the jury as their instruments in crushing a political enemy or rather they strike in his person at all their political enemies . . .'[22] The real objection to Carlile was not to his religious scepticism, which many of those most active in persecuting him shared, but to his politics. The decision to prosecute for blasphemy rather than for sedition was, then, a ruse, but, as Hunt immediately recognised, it was a very powerful one. The fastest growing popular movement in the early nineteenth century was not, despite the huge crowds that gathered to hear Henry Hunt, connected with any demand for political reform. Methodism was a movement, indeed, that had as its founder a high Tory, and continued to preach officially that political quiescence was a religious duty. In Manchester, the Methodist leadership were among the most furious of the reformers' opponents, ever anxious to expose and expel any of their membership who could be proved sympathetic to the reformers' cause. In 1819, Methodism was not remarkable for any coherent theology, it was marked rather by a loose set of tendencies, foremost among them an insistence on inner illumination, a sudden experience of conversion, and the use of the sermon, characteristically the sermon that dwelt emotionally on the reality of hell fire, to prompt such experiences. Any churchman sympathetic to these tendencies might be described as a methodist, but, in addition, the official Methodists had developed a system of organization, based on local chapels, weekly subscriptions, and field preachers travelling the country, so powerful that it was already the model for all attempts by political reformers to organize themselves across the nation. Methodism and reform were the two great popular movements in 1819, and they were rival movements. Hunt's defence of Carlile was so impassioned, because he realised that the great rival to Tom Paine as a popular ideologue was John Wesley. In London, as we find in *Peter Bell the Third*:

---

[22] *The Letters of Percy Bysshe Shelley*, 2, 143.

There is great talk of Revolution –
    And a great chance of despotism –
    German soldiers – camps – confusion –
    Tumults – lotteries – rage – delusion –
        Gin – suicide and methodism.   (172–6)

It is a list not quite so chaotic as it seems. The 'Revolution' of the first
line was most powerfully inhibited in 1819 by the 'methodism' of the
last.[23]

It is unsurprising, then, that Leigh Hunt supplemented his defence
of Carlile by various direct attacks on the Methodists. A series on
pulpit oratory is prefaced by gloomy remarks on 'the growth of
methodism'.[24] The execution of a murderer is seized on as another
striking illustration of its ill efects. Robert Dean was a particularly
notorious murderer because his victim had been a four year old girl
whose throat he had cut. At his trial, he explained that his addresses
had been refused by a young lady. He had thought to take his revenge
by killing her, but it had occurred to him that her soul might not be in
a fit state to be received into Heaven and so he had chosen to kill the
little girl instead, being assured of her innocence. As might be imagined, the Rev. Mr Mann, who attended Dean in prison, found him
particularly susceptible to religious comfort, and, in his speech before
his execution, Dean pronounced himself sure that 'Christ was waiting
for him' whereas 'such as Voltaire and Paine . . . are eternally damned

---

[23] Halevy and E. P. Thompson both argue that Methodism was the most
powerful force inhibiting political revolution in the first two decades of the
nineteenth century. More recently, their thesis has been challenged by a
number of historians who have succeeded in demonstrating that the Methodist leadership was ineffective in its attempts to control the political activities
of Methodist members. See, for example, D. Hempton, *Methodism and Politics
in British Society 1750–1830* (London, 1984). But neither Hunt nor Shelley
would have been in a position to distinguish between the pronouncements of
Methodist leaders and the practice of their membership. Southey's biography
of Wesley was not published until 1820, but he was known to be working on it,
and the information could only have strengthened the suspicion of Hunt's set
that the Lake poets and Methodists were making common cause.

[24] *The Examiner*, no. 603 (18 July 1819), 460–1. This series was not written by
Hunt, but distaste for Methodism was house policy. The best short statement
of the motives for this repugnance is given by Hazlitt in his essay, 'On the
Causes of Methodism', which was included in *The Round Table* (1817). See
The Complete Works of William Hazlitt, ed. P. P. Howe (London and Toronto,
1932), 4, 57–61.

for their impiety'. Hunt was reminded of another murderer who had
killed his girlfriend in order to remove her to 'a better world' and was
apprehended praying devoutly in a Methodist chapel. 'Methodism',
Hunt argues somewhat wildly 'has to do with these matters in two
ways: it first removes, by its frightening and threatening dogmas, the
mental barriers which nature has raised against the commission of
crime, destroying and confounding our innate sense of right and
wrong, and then, when the mischief is done, it completes its evil
effect, by forcing from its wretched victims declarations of comfort
which they cannot feel, and expectations of future happiness which
they cannot hope for'.[25]

It was in this mood that Hunt sat down to write his review of
Wordsworth's *Peter Bell*, convinced that Methodism, and the lively
fear of Hell that Methodist preachers delighted to arouse, was being
used as an instrument of political control, and convinced, too, that
such a fear was hostile not only to the cause of political reform, but to
all the pleasures of life, substituting for the loving kindness towards
one's fellows which is the condition of happiness a perverse ambition
to escape the torment which it is the lot of most of us to suffer. Given
this, it is no wonder that he found the poem a 'didactic little horror', a
'Methodistical nightmare', the story of a man brought to 'a proper
united sense of hare-bells and hell-fire' when he happens to overhear
'a Damnation Sermon, which a Methodist is vociferating'. 'The very
hope of such things as Methodism', Hunt writes 'is founded on hopelessness, and that too of the very worst sort, – namely, hopelessness of
others, and salvation for itself'. The following month, Hunt was still
sadly absorbed by the evidence *Peter Bell* seemed to give of a poet who
had lapsed into Methodistical selfishness, content to carry his 'egotism
and 'saving knowledge' about with him', ready to side with 'the oldest
tyrannies and slaveries', rendered indifferent to human misery by a
gloomy sense that most of his fellows are damned. But Hunt was now
reviewing Shelley's *Rosalind and Helen*, and he seized the opportunity
to point the contrast between the two poets. One was intent on
making men 'timid, servile, and (considering his religion) selfish', the
other intent on making them 'fearless, independent, affectionate,
infinitely social'. 'You might be made to worship a devil by the process

---

[25] *The Examiner* reported Dean's trial in no. 588 (4 April 1819), 212, and his
execution in no. 591 (25 April 1819), 259–61.

of Mr Wordsworth's philosophy,' he concludes: 'by that of Mr Shelley you might re-seat a dethroned goddess'.[26]

The review must have been read by Shelley as an invitation, and he responded to it by writing a poem in which Peter Bell dies in despair, is raised by the devil, and proudly enters into the devil's service. When he is raised from the dead, Peter loses all memory of his previous existence amongst the mountains and the lakes. Instead, he imagines that:

> he had parents dear,
> Brothers, sisters, cousins, cronies,
> In the fens o' Lincolnshire . . . (111–13)

Lincolnshire, I take it, because Lincolnshire is Wesley's county, and the true home of the poet Wordsworth had become. Peter Bell is installed as the devil's footman at his town mansion in Grosvenor Square. The poem moves to London, and in its third part, Shelley writes his own 'Damnation Sermon':

> So good and bad, sane and mad,
>   The oppressor and the oppressed;
> Those who weep to see what others
> Smile to inflict upon their brothers;
>   Lovers, haters, worst and best;
>
> All are damned . . .   (252–7)

But it is, of course, a parody of the sermon heard by Peter Bell, for we are not all damned by God – that is 'a lie' – rather we are 'damned by one another' and we damn ourselves, and the Hell to which we are consigned is not at all supernatural but only a 'city much like London'.

Peter Bell the Third counters Wordsworth's religiosity with the liberal humanism that Shelley shared with Hunt. If Shelley is more willing than he had shown himself previously to present his scepticism in a form that could readily be mistaken for a comfortably humane and

---

[26] The review appeared in *The Examiner*, no. 593 (9 May 1819), 302–3, and may well have had its effect in prompting *Peter Bell the Third*, not least by establishing Wordsworth and Shelley as opposites. The characterization of Worsworth as 'unsexual', not daring to lift nature's tunic, and averting his eyes shame-faced from her laughing gaze, may have been prompted by Hunt's tribute to the contrary quality in Shelley: 'Mr Shelley seems to look at Nature with such an earnest and intense love, that at last if she does not break her ancient silence, she returns him look for look'.

latiduninarian version of Christianity, if he leaves it possible for his reader to suppose that his objection is to the notion of a God of love who expresses himself in 'burning coals', then this only brings him closer to Hunt. The poem shares, too, Hunt's sense that such a religion, by imprisoning its exponent in a gloomy selfishness, deprives him of that pleasure in friendly society that always seemed to Hunt the highest human happiness, and infects, too, his sexual relationships. It leaves him, what Shelley calls Peter Bell, 'a solemn and unsexual man'.

Hunt's natural high spirits made it easy for him to oppose solemnity: he found it much more difficult to express his thoughts on sexuality, but during 1819 he felt insistently a need to do so. The case of Robert Dean was an unmistakable example of the perversion of the sexual instinct by a crude but powerful religious sensibility. Another notorious criminal case prompted similar thoughts. An errant wife had returned to her husband after being abandoned by her lover. The husband stabbed the wife, and it was mistakenly believed that her injuries would prove fatal. But the wife refused to say who had stabbed her, and her determined silence made her into something of a popular heroine, until some facts were revealed about the manner in which she had left her husband that rather dimmed the public's admiration of her. Hunt tells the story sadly, and represents it as 'another proof of the false moral system upon which the intercourse of the sexes is carried on'.[27] But he says no more, and the thought tails away rather lamely. Hunt was well known to hold heterodox views on the institution of marriage – indeed Blackwood's suggests that it was this that made his journal so popular amongst single young gentlemen – but he was chary of announcing them directly, and no clue as to their nature could be gleaned from his own happy, if chaotic, domestic life. Shelley's domestic arrangements were notoriously more entangled, but when Hunt wrote to defend his friend from the Quarterly's salacious attack, he tactfully side-stepped the unconventional nature of Shelley's menage. Editors of popular journals must accept constraints on their expression of unconventional views. Hunt's sturdy defence of Carlile and his outspoken contempt for hell-fire Christianity already gave ammunition to all those who wished to identify opposition to Hunt's politics with a defence of the Christian religion. It would be at the very least rash, if he were to allow his opponents to represent themselves also as the champions of family life.

[27] The Examiner, no. 606 (8 August 1819), 504.

Shelley could, and did, allow himself more freedom, but in *Peter Bell the Third* the attack on Wordsworth as 'unsexual', a 'moral eunuch', is oddly unstable in its direction. Shelley is quick to distinguish himself from fashionable rakes: 'Things whose trade is , over ladies / To lean, and flirt, and stare, and simper'. But when Wordsworth is represented as comically reverent in his dealings with Nature, daring to do no more than touch 'the hem of Nature's shift', his timidity is laughed at with the kind of hearty masculinity that one associates with Fielding. 'Tempt not again my deepest bliss', says Nature. Burns makes an appearance as a sort of poetic Tom Jones next to whom Wordsworth is revealed as a Blifil, a quotation from Boccaccio flamboyantly transforms the moon from an emblem of virginity into an emblem of sexual promise endlessly renewed, and at the last, Wordsworth is categorised with schoolboy relish, as 'a male prude', that is a male embodiment of an unpleasant and female type. These are jokes, of course: *Peter Bell the Third* is a comic poem. But when ideas are expressed comically that in other poems by Shelley – *Queen Mab*, *Laon and Cythna*, or *Prometheus Unbound* – are allowed serious expression, their character is altered, for it is characteristic of comic writing that it appeals to exactly those distinctions, between man and woman, rich and poor, the educated and the uneducated, that in other writings Shelley is at pains to deny. In *Queen Mab*, conventional views on religion and sexuality are presented as mistaken, in *Peter Bell the Third*, they are assailed as vulgar prejudices. *Queen Mab*, quite literally, is spoken from a position outside the social world, but in outer space there are no jokes. The comedy of *Peter Bell the Third* implicates the poem in the social system that it seeks to analyse.

When Shelley allows his contempt for rakes to glint from the word he uses to describe their activities, 'trade', it seems an unfortunate regression to the set of gentlemanly prejudices into which Shelley was initiated by the accident of his birth. In fact, no poem of Shelley's relies more on its appeal to its readers' awareness of class distinctions and of the comic incongruities they give rise to. We are reminded that dandies share with evangelicals the habit of oiling their hair, and are invited to savour the wide distinction made by the difference between the oils each group favours.[28] The protean character of the devil is

---

[28] Michael Scrivener, in one of the most intelligent readings of *Peter Bell the Third*, points out the poem's 'social snobbery', and its indulgence in aristocratic

pointed by the incongruity of his being able to appear now as a lord
with a mansion in Grosvenor Square, and now as 'a slop-merchant',
that is, a dealer in cheap ready-made clothes, from Wapping.
Wordsworth is ridiculed by being represented in the guise of a footman, dressed in livery, and humbly waiting behind his master's chair at
table. The comedy of his being placed in this menial station is heightened by the presence of Coleridge at the table as a guest. Shelley, like
Reynolds, the author of 'the ante-natal Peter', makes play of the
disparity between Peter's 'individual mind', to which he pays noble
tribute, and the comically humdrum materials on which it feeds:
ditches, fences, milk pans and pails, pedlars and old parsons. Nothing
is more cockney in *Peter Bell the Third* than its social unease, its
embarrassed difficulty in placing itself within the class system that by
1819 had pervaded British life and British politics.

Unlike Shelley, Hunt was vulnerable to snobbish attack, and very
often the object of it. He was, after all, the leader of 'the cockney
School of Poetry', and the cockney poets were from the first defined in
relation to their social class. They were poetasters who lacked the
advantage of a university education, and whose productions could, on
that account, always be dismissed as 'vulgar'. In some moods Hunt
could take delight in his own social status: it was the ground upon
which he built his most substantial achievement, the invention of
suburbia as the locus for a literary and aesthetic system of values. But
in 1819 class antagonisms reached a pitch that made it impossible for
him to accommodate himself gracefully to the ambivalence of his own
social position. Whenever, in these months, he is forced to confront
the question of class in the pages of *The Examiner*, he betrays embar-
rassment. He wishes that Henry Hunt would be 'a little less coarse',
and immediately and inconsequentially adds that 'the charge of coar-
seness itself is contemptible from the mouths of his aristocratical
enemies'. He upbraids the editor of the *Courier* for attempting to
discredit the reformers by describing them as 'tradesmen', but himself
repeatedly claims that the *Courier*'s editor began life as a tailor, and
Gifford of the *Quarterly* had been an apprentice shoemaker.[29] Like

'sneers' and 'jibes' at the merely bourgeois. See *Radical Shelley: The Philosophical
Anarchism and Utopian Thought of Percy Bysshe Shelley* (Princeton, 1982), 218–
24.
[29] *The Examiner*, no. 610 (5 September 1819), 561–2. See also the leading
article, 'More Absurdities of the Courier Respecting the Trades of the Reformers &c', in no. 614 (3 October 1819) where Hunt vitiates his earnest appeal

Shelley in *Peter Bell* he is morbidly sensitive to the social distinctions he affects to despise, and the consequence is to muddy the clarity of his political thinking.

By 1819, it had become impossible to describe political life except in terms of class division. The salient fact, observed by almost all commentators, was the emergence of what Shelley calls in *A Philosophical View of Reform* 'a fourth class' which no longer accepted that 'its interests were sensibly interwoven with that of those who enjoyed a constitutional presence', a new class unwilling to recognize the Whigs as its 'natural leaders', and increasingly unsure whether it was willing to be represented by aristocratic radicals such as Burdett, or Shelley himself. It is this class to which Shelley addresses himself in a poem such as *The Mask of Anarchy*, but it is a class that he can address only if he will consent to speak in disguise. In *Peter Bell the Third*, it is Shelley's awareness of the 'fourth class', and of his ambivalent relationship with it, that is the driving force of the poem, for it is the new existence of this class that made Wordsworth's decision to publish *Peter Bell* in 1819 so disturbing.

The writer who had done more than any other to bring this 'fourth class' into being was William Cobbett. In *The Examiner* Hunt had consistently voiced his antagonism to Cobbett, but in 1819 he began cautiously to modify his position, qualifying his disagreement with many of Cobbett's opinions by paying large compliments to his prose and to the educative value of his journalism.[30] Again Shelley's attitudes went in tandem. Peacock sent copies of the *Political Register* to Shelley in Italy, but in January 1819 Shelley was prompted only to regret 'that so powerful a genius should be combined with the most odious moral qualities'. By July, he wrote to Peacock: 'Cobbett still more & more delights me, with all my horror of the sanguinary commonplaces of his creed'. He took particular pleasure in Cobbett's 'puff-out', his scheme to disrupt the national economy by the random distribution of forged bank notes.[31] Just as revealingly, Cobbett begins

for the dignity and utility of the practice of trade by repeating his jibes at Gifford and the proprietor of the *Courier*.

[30] For example in *The Examiner*, of 5 September 1819, Hunt writes of Cobbett: 'with all our dislike of him on some accounts, he is at once the most powerful as well as popular political writer now living' (no. 610, 561–2). Hunt relied very largely on an appeal to the educative power of Cobbett's writings to rebut the argument that the lower orders were too ignorant to be allowed a vote.

[31] *The Letters of Percy Bysshe Shelley*, 2, 75 and 99.

to leave his mark on Shelley's prose, tightening its formal periods until Shelley can reproduce the sharp, derisive epigrams that salt Cobbett's style. 'Monarchy', Shelley writes in A *Philosophical View of Reform*, 'is just the string that ties the robber's bundle'. This is not prose well adapted to refined warnings that the reformers must on all accounts eschew violence: it is prose that creates its own momentum, drawing Shelley on to rehearse sentiments that seem indistinguishable from the 'sanguinary commonplaces' he regretted in Cobbett. 'So dear is power', he warns, 'that the tyrants themselves neither then, nor now, nor ever, left or leave a path to freedom but through their own blood'. Alternatively, Shelley imagines the opponents of reform in the Commons struck with 'blindness and confusion', yielding to a 'radiant and irresistible force' in the shape of petitions 'severally written by Godwin, Hazlitt, Bentham, and Hunt'. There is no connection between these two positions. The one represents Old Corruption as a power that must be overthrown, the other presents it as an argument that may be refuted. In one view the only effective agent of reform is the concerted action of the people, the 'many', whose power the 'few' will be unable to resist; in the other, the tyrants yield to superior argument, and the revolution may be bloodlessly achieved by the presentation to the House of Commons of some pamphlets written by the 'feelosofers'. A *Philosophical View of Reform* collapses under the strain of its own incoherence – but it ends by warning its reader against the influence of 'certain vulgar agitators', foremost amongst whom, as Shelley well knew, was Cobbett.

In *Peter Bell the Third*, Shelley borrows from Cobbett his description of the National Debt as 'a scheme of paper money', but otherwise his concern is to warn against any indulgence in 'Cobbett's snuff, revenge'. His tactic is to represent Cobbett and the 'vulgar agitators' as if they were in league with the perpetrators of the Peterloo massacre and the ministry that had congratulated them on their staunchness. In London:

> There is a Castles and a Canning,
> A Cobbett and a Castlereagh ...   (152–3)

The informer and agent provocateur, Castles,[32] the ministers, and Cobbett, it is suggested, are morally equivalent and practically in

---

[32] For an account of Castle's activities, see E. P. Thompson, *The Making of the English Working Classes*, 534, 537–9, and 693–6.

league, engaged in a single conspiracy against the peace of the nation. The lines affect an even-handed distaste for either extreme, but such declarations of liberal fair-mindedness are often the last refuge of those who find themselves bewildered. Cobbett and Castlereagh take their place within a London represented by Shelley as the site only of a vast confusion, in which the poet sits forlorn, preserving his faith that somehow 'this ugly Hell' may be made into 'a Heaven', but with no notion as to what kind of machinery would be required to effect such a transformation.

Cobbett is one of two powerfully ambivalent figures who preoccupied Shelley at this time; the other, and for *Peter Bell the Third* the more important, is of course Wordsworth. Shelley clung to the still conventional view of Wordsworth as a poet who had sold his principles for a pension, as a poet who had once found his deepest imaginative sympathies with the poor and dispossessed and now grounded his self-esteem on his occupation of a house with a 'genteel drive' neatly laid with 'sifted gravel'. Wordsworth's decision to publish *Peter Bell* in 1819 could only have worked to shake this glib assessment. It was a poem, as Wordsworth insisted to the unrestrained amusement of the reviewers, that he had carried with him for twenty-one years, that is, ever since 1798, the year of the first publication of *Lyrical Ballads*. The preface to *Peter Bell* was surely written as a defiant rebuttal of readers such as Shelley, as a public declaration that he remained the poet he had been, unchanged in all essentials from the youthful poet that his younger contemporaries professed to admire. The poem itself is equally unsettling. Reynolds, in parodying it, simply expresses his vulgar amusement that poems should be written about people with plebeian names. *Peter Bell* is associated in his derision with early poems such as *Goody Blake and Harry Gill* and *The Idiot Boy*, with the odd result that the young London radical appears trivially snobbish in comparison with the poet he is attempting to ridicule. Shelley is similarly wrong-footed. His reference to Wordsworth's 'genteel drive' swithers uncertainly between radical contempt for the earnings of placemen and aristocratic scorn for bourgeois gentrification. *Peter Bell* with its simple ballad metre, its severely unadorned language, and, most important, its subject is a demonstration that Wordsworth's muse remained 'a levelling one'. Such a demonstration could only have been disconcerting to Shelley, transforming Wordsworth from an opponent who could be confronted into 'a walking paradox'.

Shelley includes in his poem a parody of the most notorious lines that Wordsworth ever composed, lines that formed part of

Wordsworth's *Thanksgiving Ode* after the defeat of Napoleon at Water-loo. Hunt had quoted one of those lines – 'carnage is his daughter' – in his first report of the Peterloo massacre, ascribing the sentiment to 'a pathetic court poet'. It was easy to understand what had prompted him to remember Wordsworth's poem, for Peterloo was given its name in response to a remark made by one of the militiamen who was survey-ing the scene after the killing and overheard by a reporter: 'This is our Waterloo.' Wordsworth's phrase was already well known before Hunt invoked it: it concluded the paragraph in which Hazlitt had famously indicted poetry as an 'aristocratical faculty' animated by 'a very anti-levelling principle'. But Hunt repeated the quotation a few months after Wordsworth had published *Peter Bell*, a poem of exactly the kind that would prompt Hazlitt to identify Wordsworth as the one poet invulnerable to his general charge, as the one poet of whom it could be said that 'his muse is a levelling one'.[33] On the one hand, Wordsworth was a poet who could be identified with Sidmouth, Castlereagh and Canning, and with all those who had colluded in the Manchester massacre. On the other, he was the one writer who had achieved in poetry something like what Cobbett had achieved in prose.

Surprisingly, it is the second possibility that Shelley develops. In a note appended to his parody of the *Thanksgiving Ode* Wordsworth is described as 'a sort of metrical Cobbett'. Shelley notes that both men will be equally affronted by the comparison, but insists that it is an instance of a general truth: 'It is curious to observe how often extremes meet'. It is not so much curious as a smug cliché, its fragile foundation Shelley's contention that both men are alike in the 'sanguinary com-monplaces of their creed'. It leaves the suspicion that Cobbett and Wordsworth are more disturbingly related for Shelley than he cares to realise. It is not simply that both are men whose opinions are dis-figured by their willingness to accept violence, nor that both are men of genius deformed by perverted moral instincts. Wordsworth and

---

[33] Hunt quotes the phrase from Wordsworth in *The Examiner*, no. 608 (22 August 1819), 530. Hazlitt uses it to clinch his assertion that poetry is in its nature undemocratic in the essay on *Coriolanus* in his *The Characters of Shakes-peare's Plays* (1817). Wordsworth's Muse is described by Hazlitt as 'levelling' in the essay on Wordsworth in *The Spirit of the Age* (1825). See *The Complete Works of William Hazlitt*, 4, 214, and 11, 87. The offending lines were removed from the poem by Wordsworth for the edition of 1845. They are preserved by de Selincourt in his edition of *The Poetical Works of William Wordsworth* (Ox-ford, 1946), 3, 461–2.

Cobbett are associated as writers that Shelley can neither accept nor reject, writers that leave him uneasy, and part of his discomfort arises from his recognition that Wordsworth with his instinctive under-standing of the power of a methodist sermon, and Cobbett with his equally instinctive understanding of popular radicalism had access to modes of feeling and to kinds of language from which Shelley, by his class as much as by his thinking, was debarred.

Peter Bell the Third is a poem in which identities fracture. Peter Bell, himself, as Shelley notes at the outset, is not one but three, created by Wordsworth, anticipated by Reynolds, and revived by Shelley, and within Shelley's own poem Peter repeatedly changes identities as he is transported from the Lakes to London before being restored to his native Westmoreland. Even his name once changes, to 'P.Verbovale Esq'. He changes, of course, because Wordsworth is a turncoat, the erstwhile radical who has degenerated into a 'pathetic court poet', the poet of the poor who has taken a house with a 'genteel drive' and occupied himself by defending the right of Lord Lansdowne to treat Westmoreland as his own borough.[34] But he changes, too, because he is the object both of Shelley's contempt and of his admiration, and because in Peter Bell's fractured identity Shelley recognizes a grotesque reflection of himself. The parody of the *Thanksgiving Ode* for a few lines diverges from its model, and when it does something rather odd happens:

> Slash them at Manchester,
> Glasgow, Leeds and Chester;
> Drench all with blood from Avon to Trent
>
> Let thy body-guard yeomen
> Hew down men and women.
> And laugh with bold triumph till Heaven be rent! (644–9)

It is almost as if Shelley has drifted into a parody of a poem he had written himself a few weeks before:

> And if then the tyrants dare
> Let them ride among you there,

---

[34] Peter Bell's yellowness is not chosen simply as a colour appropriately sulphureous. Yellow was characteristically preferred in the livery of footmen, as in Thackeray's *Yellowplush Papers*, and it may be, too, that Shelley remembered that yellow was the colour of the Lansdowne interest in the Westmoreland election of 1818, when it was opposed to the blue of Brougham's supporters.

> Slash, and stab, and maim, and hew, –
> What they like, that let them do.
>   (*The Mask of Anarchy*, 340–3)

Is this Shelley parodying a poem by 'Peter Bell', or 'Peter Bell' parodying a poem by Shelley? The effect is at its most intense when Peter becomes the butt of the reviewers, who have been bribed by the devil to abuse him. He is charged with a catalogue of grotesque offences, that appear to have in common only their comical outrageousness. But consider the mildest of the charges:

> What does the rascal mean or hope,
> No longer imitating Pope,
>   In that barbarian Shakespeare poking? (475–7)

This is an imaginary accusation as levelled at Wordsworth, but an accurate summary of the kind of ridicule that Hunt had invited by his preface to *Foliage*. A stanza that Shelley thought better of tells how Peter was hailed as an 'impious libertine' who 'commits incest with his sister / In ruined Abbies'. Shelley scored out this stanza, surely, because he feared that Byron might not be amused by it.[35] Another reviewer exclaims:

> Is incest not enough,
> And must there be adultery too?
> Grace after meat? (478–80)

The imaginary attack on Wordsworth is unnervingly close to John Taylor Coleridge's attack on *Laon and Cythna*.[36] Coleridge, in that same review, hinted at his knowledge of the painful personal events that had led to Shelley's leaving England. It is hard not to think that

---

[35] This stanza was first published by F. W. Bateson, 'Shelley on Wordsworth: Two Unpublished Stanzas from *Peter Bell the Third*', *Essays in Criticism*, 17 (1967), 125–9. Bateson wonders whether the stanza might indicate that Shelley shared his own suspicions concerning the relationship between William and Dorothy, but this seems wholly unlikely.

[36] These lines are modelled on a passage, evidently referring to Shelley, in the *Quarterly*'s review of Hunt's *Foliage*: 'he, if such there be, who thinks even adultery vapid unless he can render it more exquisitely poignant by adding incest to it'. (*The Quarterly Review*, 18 (January 1818), 328.

those same events were in Shelley's mind when he devised the most fantastic of all the reviewers' charges:

> Peter seduced Mrs. Foy's daughter,
> Then drowned the Mother in Ullswater,
> The last thing as he went to bed.   (470–2)

I do not believe that Shelley could have written those lines without thinking of the daughter of another famous woman, and of another mother, drowned not in Ullswater but in the Serpentine, and to think of such things is to transform the lines – comic high spirits evaporate leaving a residue of hysterical bitterness, and Wordsworth becomes not the butt of Shelley's attack, but a fellow victim, as much a casualty of a national mood in which taste in poetry had become simply an expression of political partisanship as Hunt, Keats, Byron and Shelley himself.

Peter Bell the Third begins by dividing the poets of England into two opposing ranks, but in the reviewers' attacks the lines are broken, and the poem does not allow them to re-form. Peter, in his final transformation, is defined by his lack of all definition:

> He was no Whig, he was no Tory:
> No Atheist and no Christian he, –
> He got so subtle that to be
> Nothing was all his glory.   (565–8)[37]

He is reduced to one single belief, that 'happiness is wrong', and he feeds his imagination by gazing raptly on scenes of violence, of pain and of death. He remains the opposite of that other poet, placed by the poem in London and conventionally identified with Shelley himself:

> And some few, like we know who,
> Damned – but God alone knows why –
> To believe their minds are given

---

[37] Reiman and Powers follow other editors in reading 'deist' rather than 'atheist', but in Mary Shelley's fair copy of the poem, as Reiman indicates in his edition of it, 'atheist' is scored out, 'deist' substituted, and then 'deist', too, is scored out. This must mean either that Shelley had reverted to his first thought, or that he had decided that neither word was satisfactory. In the circumstances it seems better to read 'atheist', which, to my ear, gives a better line.

> To make this ugly Hell a Heaven;
>   In which faith they live and die.   (242–6)

But *Peter Bell the Third* is a poem set in dark times, and in such times even the most striking differences can be obscured , in the dark 'None knows a pigeon from a crow' (251).

   The Mask of Anarchy and *Peter Bell the Third* are Shelley's two most substantial responses to England in 1819, and one part of their interest is that the responses are so different. In *The Mask of Anarchy* Shelley records how the events of that year have made one duty paramount, the duty to take sides. In the other, those same events, looked at differently, make taking sides impossible. They leave a public writer with the choice of agreeing with Cobbett or agreeing with Wordsworth, and that for Shelley is an impossible dilemma: he can accept neither, he can reject neither, and even if he could make such a choice it would not help, for he recognizes that he can become neither. In the one poem the nation is marshalled into those two ranks that had confronted each other in St Peter's Field, in the other the nation is best represented by its capital, by the city of London, as a confusion too vast to comprehend.

Ahasuerus-Xerxes:
Hellas as Allegory of Dissemination

EDWARD LARRISSY

It was Edward Dowden who first argued that the unfinished Prologue
to *Hellas* was a reversion to the idea behind the project for a lyrical
drama based on the Book of Job.[1] This had originally been meditated
in the period that led up to the composition of *Prometheus Unbound*.[2]
As Carlos Baker reasonably conjectures, 'Shelley's deep dislike of the
concept of the Old Testament God would perhaps have prompted him
to treat the subject somewhat in the manner of *Prometheus Unbound*,
with Job as protagonist and Jahweh as the equivalent of Jupiter'.[3] But
there is a particular nuance in Job that Shelley would wish to exploit;
one that Blake had arguably been exploiting for many years, though it
was not until 1810, at the earliest, that he began to work on a series of
designs for the whole story.[4] Eventually, of course, Blake's labours
would bear fruit in the extraordinary *Illustrations of the Book of Job*
(1826).

The nuance I have in mind is present in the facts which link the
Prologue to *Hellas* with Job. In the former, the herald of Eternity
announces 'It is the day when all the sons of God/Wait in the roofless
senate-house, whose floor/Is chaos . . .' (Prologue, 1–3). Among the
sons of God, apart from Christ and Mahomet, is Satan. In the Book of
Job (I:7), we are told: 'Now there was a day when the sons of God
came to present themselves before the Lord, and Satan came also
among them.' The connection is surely beyond a doubt. The point
Shelley would have wished to emphasize is the apparent collusion

Note: Quotations from Shelley are taken from *Shelley: Poetical Works*, ed.
Thomas Hutchinson, new edn corrected by G. M. Matthews (London, 1970),
referred to in the text as H.

[1]   Edward Dowden, *The Life of Percy Bysshe Shelley*, 2nd edn (London, 1896),
p. 410.
[2]   The original plan is referred to in Mary Shelley's notes on *Prometheus
Unbound*.
[3]   Carlos Baker, *Shelley's Major Poetry: The Fabric of a Vision* (Princeton,
1948), p. 121.
[4]   Andrew Wright, *Blake's Job: A Commentary* (Oxford, 1972), p. xvi.

between God and Satan, when Satan suggests that Job's piety will not withstand the trial of misfortune (I:9–11). God consents to Satan's testing Job, replying, 'Behold all that he hath is in thy power' (I:12). The interest this scene would have evinced for Shelley is in the way it could be seen as providing a concise mythical rendering of the notion that God puts humanity to an impossible test, and then punishes them for failing it. As the notes to *Hellas* put it, 'a Power, who tempted, betrayed, and punished the innocent beings who were called into existence by His sole will' (H 480). A similar conception is conveyed by Blake's *Illustrations*, especially the second, depicting Satan before the throne of God.[5] The fact that Job happens to pass the test would not have diminished the story's appeal for Shelley: quite the contrary.

A less obvious point, but one which is implied by Shelley, is the way in which a God who counts Satan as one of his sons can be seen as morally indifferent, and as conforming to a conception at some points comparable to that of an amoral Necessity. Satan, Christ and Mahomet put their points of view about the way the battle between Greeks and Turks should go, and about how the 'Father' will ordain 'destiny' to operate. But though Christ is clearly Shelley's approved figure, neither he nor the others are supplied with the sense of having a special lien on Destiny. Further, Satan and Mahomet fail to live up to the simply malevolent roles one might half expect for them. Satan is given a development of the collusion idea when he says to Destiny: 'Go, thou Viceregent of my will, no less/Than of The Father's' (142–3). This initiates a passages in which he exults in the prospect not only of 'Superstition', 'War', and 'Fraud', but also of 'Famine', 'Pestilence' and (most all-encompassing) 'Change' (144–50). In other words, here we have a fairly typical example of Shelley's tendency to mix bad-mindedness and bad luck. But the fact that it is Satan who has so much bad luck to look after tends to reduce his darkness a shade or two, so that he approximates a mere prince of misfortune. In line with this interpretation he is unexpectedly disinterested as regards the outcome of the Greek war of liberation. His main concern is that suffering should continue whatever happens. There is an implicit assurance in his words that it will. Addressing Destiny, he remarks:

> be mine
> Thy trophies, whether Greece again become

---

5   Ibid., p. 8, reproduction.

The fountain in the desert whence the earth
Shall drink of freedom, which shall give it strength
To suffer, or a gulf of hollow death
To swallow all delight, all life, all hope.   (136–41)

Shelley's Satan, then, is fairly neutral with respect to the brief political
and moral excitements of Earth. He is far more interested in the long
and sorry tale of suffering and mutability. And this suggests that
Shelley's interest lies there too ('Oh, cease! must hate and death
return?'). So the treatment of Satan supports Milton Wilson's judgment that Shelley's stress on the Platonic undermines his ostensible
interest in the topical 'radical' issue.[6]

In pursuit of this conclusion, Wilson makes a good point about
Mahomet's speech in the Prologue. Mahomet cries, 'Be thou a curse on
them whose creed/Divides and multiplies the most high God' (178–9).
Wilson remarks: 'Shelley, no less than Mahomet, was opposed to the
conception of the Trinity.'[7] And he astutely notes that Mahomet
might have been employed, in a complete prologue, not only as a
supporter of tyrants, but as 'an instrument for criticizing the short-
comings of Christianity.'[8] Mahomet's reference to 'Christian night'
(171) would be congenial enough to Shelley, as to Gibbon, who is
quoted in the notes (H 479). There is probably more to it than that,
however. While it is true that Shelley's 'One' might be better represented by Allah than by the Trinity, it is questionable whether
Hassan's supposedly Muslim conception of 'one God, one King, one
Hope, one Law', referred to in the play proper (Hellas 333), has
Shelley's loyalty. The notion smacks of tyranny, like Blake's 'One
King, one God, one Law' (Book of Urizen, plate 4, line 40). So while it
is probably true that Shelley would have liked to smuggle criticism of
Christian theology into the Prologue, under the guise of Muslim
philosophizing, the Muslims are themselves victims of a tendency to
forget that in this world we cannot gain a sense of the One save
through the partial forms which 'transfuse' it (Adonais, 468).[9] And this
is one of the meanings of Hellas, as I hope will become clearer. But as

6 Milton Wilson, Shelley's Later Poetry (New York, 1959), p. 186.
7 Ibid., p. 184.
8 Ibid.
9 Earl R. Wasserman, 'Shelley's Last Poetics: A Reconstruction', From Sensi-
bilty to Romanticism: Essays Presented to Frederick A. Pottle, ed. Frederick W.
Hilles and Harold Bloom (New York, 1965), pp. 488–90.

to the Prologue, it is perhaps sufficiently obvious that it sets up no certainties, and that it undoes all the oppositions which it pretends to proffer as a means of understanding. Christ, bereft of his special relationship with the Father, pleads for Greece; Satan, not greatly concerned which way this particular battle goes, hopes that suffering will continue to yield a rich harvest; and Mahomet, the victim of a distorted truth, understandably wishes to see the defeat of Christian ignorance and superstition. Shelley has philosophical reasons for disavowing any affiliation to simple notions of the truth, and for doubts as to whether the liberation of Greece will entail the resurrection of Hellas: in context the choice of name is significant of the eternal Greece and its values. But, in passing, one should not rule out the possibility that he may have been encouraged in scepticism about the Greek struggle by his knowledge of the actual train of events in 1821.

The uprising in Wallachia had been fomented by the leader of the Greek 'Friendly Society', Alexander Hypselantes. He was a scion of the Phanariote Greek nobility of Moldavia and Wallachia: that is to say, he came of a local ruling caste which was detested and regarded as tyrannical by its Rumanian subjects.[10] For this reason, most of the Rumanian nationalists distanced themselves from the Greeks, fatally weakening the effort in Wallachia.[11] When a battalion of young Greeks was massacred by the Turks at Dragashani, in June 1821, Hypselantes fled to Austria, where he was arrested and imprisoned.[12] The Greek leader in Moldavia followed this noble example, and fled to Russia, while most of his soldiers, after demonstrations of great heroism, were slaughtered at Skuleni.[13]

If one asks what Shelley most probably knew about these events, one should look to The Examiner, which he received regularly. From its pages it can be seen that he would have known not only about the cynical behaviour of the Great Powers, but also about the brutality which characterized the behaviour of the Greeks, no less than Turks. Thus The Examiner of 10 June 1821 informs us that the Greeks cut the throats of 'all the Mahometan inhabitants' of a town (p. 354). On 9 September we learn that 'three Jews', who had acted as guides for the Turks, 'fell into the hands of the Greeks, who nailed them to the cross,

[10] William Miller, The Ottoman Empire and Its Successors 1801–1927 (London, 1966), p. 66.
[11] Ibid., p. 68.
[12] Ibid.
[13] Ibid., p. 69.

after having torn the skin from their bodies, and exercised on them other barbarities.' (p. 565) Such were the gleams of hope that Shelley's play had to celebrate, or feed, after its fashion. Small wonder, perhaps, if he decided to entrust most of his hopes to the prospect of a revived Hellas of the mind, and if, in doing so, he should seek to compromise any *idées fixes* the reader might entertain about the supposed antagonists in this historical drama.

The play proper begins with a chorus of Greek Captive Women singing ambiguous lullabies to the sleeping Sultan in Istanbul. But their own strophes alternate with two verses provided by an Indian slave, whose sex is unspecified, and who is therefore probably male. Why an Indian? In order to emphasize the oriental ambience of Sultan Mahmud's court: for this purpose an Indian does very well, better than a Levantine. Nor are the associations thus evoked in any way malign, at least not for that Shelley who situated Prometheus's ordeal in 'the Indian Caucasus', because in that locale civilization was thought to have its origin. 'Asia' was the name of the nymph whose love fortified the Titan's sufferings, for the oriental is, in this period, associated with, among other things, desire and passionately devoted love, as numerous examples, including the works of Byron, attest. That it might also be associated with a number of other qualities, including reckless courage, treachery, cruelty and vindictiveness, is not to our purpose here. The Indian slave is devoted to the Sultan, and would even seek his own misery, 'So thou mightst win one hour of quiet sleep' (*Hellas*, 26). If Mahmud is capable of inspiring such devotion, perhaps he is not all bad. The Greek lullabies are more ambiguous, suggesting a desire for Mahmud's death: 'Be thy sleep/Calm and deep,/Like theirs who fell' (5–7). Yet at the same time they do attempt efficient lulling, including the strewing of 'opiate flowers'. The proximity of the Indian's chant helps to impart a soothing air to the whole scene. Furthermore, it reminds us that in this period Greece, as part of the European Ottoman Empire, was not clearly distinguished from the Orient in western minds. The Greek women strew flowers 'stripped from Orient bowers' (3), and the ruins of Greece are said to glow 'Like Orient mountains lost in day' (85). We are, further, entitled to draw inferences from the presence of captive women so close to a Sultan's pillow, and even, granted certain assumptions about the Orient, from the presence of an Indian boy. The total impression, since the conceptual component in all this is not very strong, is one of ambivalent desire, an ambivalence aided by the erosion of distinctions between Greeks and Orientals. In fact, even the songs of the Indian slave are ambivalent, for he wishes the Sultan a sleep 'Soft as love, and calm as death' (12), before going on to wish his own joy dead. These songs point to desire's delicious but problematic implication in circuits of domination and submission, rather than to any easy political response to despotism. They suggest, indeed, that despotism is related to some deep and cherished flaw in the human psyche. A chorus of women might lead one to posit a connection between this flaw and sexuality. But while it is typical of Shelley to give the lyric of desire to women, he undermines any simple attribution of gender characteristics by the addition of the Indian slave.[14]

After the lullabies comes a rousing though relatively uncomplicated chorus about the progress of Freedom from Greece, through the Italian city-states, to modern protestant nations ('Florence, Albion, Switzerland': 63), and thence to America and the rest of Europe, and so back to Greece: a geographical as well as temporal cycle. The next striking idea is provided by the description of Ahasuerus, the ancient Jewish visionary, whose character is described to Mahmud by Hassan in a memorable passage which, as George Bornstein points out, was one of Yeats's sacred texts.[15] The Yeatsian connection is instructive about Shelley. Yeats, of course, valued the sense of a history composed of cycles in a passage of Hassan's speech from which he half-borrowed a line for 'Sailing to Byzantium':

> from his eye looks forth
> A life of unconsumèd thought which pierces
> The Present, and the Past, and the To-come.
> Some say that this is he whom the great prophet
> Jesus, the son of Joseph, for his mockery,
> Mocked with the curse of immortality.
> Some feign that he is Enoch: others dream
> He was pre-adamite and has survived
> Cycles of generation and of ruin.   (146–54)

It is this sense of immemorial cycles of existence, moving from generation to decay, which, I believe, most interested Shelley, and which

[14] On desire and the female in Shelley, see Laura Claridge, 'The Bifurcated Female Space of Desire: Shelley's Confrontation with Language and Silence', *Out of Bounds: Male Writers and Gender(ed) Criticism*, ed. Laura Claridge and Elizabeth Langland (Amherst, 1990), pp. 92–109.

[15] George Bornstein, *Yeats and Shelley* (Chicago and London, 1970), pp. 99–102.

provides the motive force for the superb chorus which follows this scene:

> Worlds on worlds are rolling ever
>   From creation to decay,
> Like the bubbles on a river
>   Sparkling, bursting, borne away.   (197–200)

Ronald Tetreault draws attention to the connection between these lines and those in *The Triumph of Life* where the speaker grows weary of the replacement of old metaphors by new:[16]

> 'Let them pass,'
> I cried, 'the world and its mysterious doom
>
> 'Is not so much more glorious than it was,
> That I desire to worship those who drew
> New figures on its false and fragile glass
>
> 'As the old faded.'   (243–8)

But Rousseau points out that the replacement is part of a process of constant creation and decay; inadequate, time-conditioned metaphors, constantly attempting, and bravely failing, to encompass Truth:

> 'Figures ever new
> Rise on the bubble, paint them as you may;
> We have but thrown, as those before us threw,
>
> 'Our shadows on it as it passed away . . .'   (248–51)

Tetreault notes that it is hard to tell how to regard Rousseau's attitude to figuration, but that in *Hellas* the same imagery of bubbles, creation and decay 'can project an alternative to despair'.[17] The chorus 'Worlds on worlds' continues:

> But they are still immortal
> Who, through birth's orient portal

---

16 Ronald Tetreault, 'Shelley: Style and Substance', *The New Shelley: Later Twentieth-Century Views*, ed. G. Kim Blank (Basingstoke and London, 1991), p. 26.
17 Ibid.

And death's dark chasm hurrying to and fro,
  Clothe their unceasing flight
  In the brief dust and light
Gathered around their chariots as they go;
  New shapes they still may weave,
  New gods, new laws receive,
Bright or dim are they as the robes they last
  On Death's bare ribs had cast   (201–10)

These immortals are ready to create meanings as they go, and the value of these meanings is in direct proportion to the energy invested in their creation: this is surely the sense of the lines about the 'brief dust and light' thrown up by the chariot-wheels, as it is of the final lines, which, in effect, say that meanings are as 'bright' as you make them.

What are 'Death's bare ribs'? The connotations of rigid and unmoving structure are important. It is these, one may recall, which vitiate the Islamic sense of the one god. 'Death's scroll' (1079) in the final chorus, is only black and white, a writing of fixed oppositions. And the rest of this chorus explains how the fixity is constituted: by the alternation of good and evil, freedom and slavery, love and hate', which is summed up in the movement from a renewed Golden Age (1090) to the possibility that this will be followed, as before, by the return of evil:

  Oh, cease! must hate and death return?
    Cease! must men kill and die?
  Cease! drain not to its dregs the urn
    Of bitter prophecy.
  The world is weary of the past,
  Oh, might it die or rest at last!   (1096–1101)

There is a link between the constancy of this depressing binary opposition and the rigid belief in one God and law. The nature of this link is adumbrated by Mahmud in his conversation with Ahasuerus. Mahmud praises the Jew's abilities, including the fact that his spirit sees 'how man became/The monarch and the slave of this low sphere,/And all its narrow circles' (748–50). The belief in the tyrannical and vengeful God, whether Jupiter (Saturn's successor), Jehovah or Allah, goes with the master-slave relationship. It also goes with the grand opposition between good and evil, defined rigidly and prescriptively. For with a God such as this, humanity is constantly either overreaching itself in self-ignorant idealism, or despairingly wallowing in its own pre-ordained worthlessness and evil. In response Ahasuerus speaks of the changeless One in terms (768–9) which at first might suggest a reversion to pessimism, and a rejection of life. But life then receives a very full and almost rhapsodic treatment:

> Earth and ocean,
> Space, and the isles of life or light that gem
> The sapphire floods of interstellar air,
> This firmament pavilioned upon chaos,
> With all its cressets of immortal fire ... (769–73)

The idea of 'bubbles' returns, however, in scarcely pleasing guise: all the phenomena of this world are 'motes of a sick eye, bubbles and dreams' (781). Thought is the one reality (782). But the last line of this speech, in uniting thought and feeling, and giving a creative role to that union, returns us to the perspective of 'Worlds on worlds': 'Nought is but that which feels itself to be' (785).

Ahasuerus, accordingly, finds phenomena sufficiently pliable to consciousness, as he makes clear in showing how easy it is for Mahmud to call up what would appear to be the ghost of his illustrious predecessor, Mahomet II, the conqueror of Byzantium. Shelley's note describes Ahasuerus as 'tempting Mahmud to that state of mind in which ideas may be supposed to assume the force of sensations through the confusion of thought with the objects of thought, and the excess of passion animating the creations of imagination'. (H 479) But the ability to do this may end by eroding the borders of identity, in confusing the thinker himself with the objects of thought. In any case, it does seem that there is a part of each of us which transcends mere identity, for Ahasuerus speaks of Mahmud's being able to 'commune with/That portion of thyself which was ere thou/Didst start for this brief race whose crown is death' (854–6). In fact, the purpose is also to commune with his ancestor Mahomet II. But the name Mahomet, as Shelley would have known, is merely another form of Mahmud. And both forms derive from the name of the prophet, he who spoke in the Prologue. The effect is that of naming the stages of a principle or idea, rather than the characteristics of individual identities. Unexpected support for this interpretation is to be found in the Phantom's prophecy of the re-birth of Islam:

> Islam must fall, but we will reign together
> Over its ruins in the world of death:–

> And if the trunk be dry, yet shall the seed
> Unfold itself even in the shape of that
> Which gathers birth in its decay.   (887–91)

This certainly implies that Islam is corrupt, and sorts with the notion that it is misconceived, rather than radically evil. But it seems that another Islam shall arise, purged, no doubt, of some or all of its excesses. But if of all, then in what respect does it differ from the ideal Hellas? In no respect, I would suggest.

Ahasuerus is well suited to the conjuring of past existences. He himself has been through so many cycles, and possibly been so many people. But Shelley has deliberately suppressed one obvious former identity for him. The various mentions of his name in the Old Testament refer not to a Jew, but to a king of Persia. Whether all these references are to the same king or different ones is not entirely clear. But the most celebrated account of an Ahasuerus is to be found in the Book of Esther, which comes just before the Book of Job. If Shelley had been refreshing his memory of Job for the 'sons of God' passage, he need only have looked at the previous page to find the name Ahasuerus. One well-supported conjecture as to the identity of Ahasuerus in Esther makes him that Xerxes who figures in Aeschylus's *Persae*, which is, of course, the chief model for *Hellas*.[18] As Xerxes to the ancient Greeks, so Mahmud to the modern; as the ghost of Darius to Xerxes, so the Phantom of Mahomet II to Mahmud.

It is, of course, unexpected to find Shelley's Ahasuerus to any degree identified with the tyrant Xerxes. Yet the accumulation of evidence is so strong that it might be deemed to put the matter beyond chance: it would certainly be a coincidence if Shelley had unknowingly included in the play an alternative name for one of its chief

---

[18] For a brief summary of such conjecture about the identity of the Biblical Ahasuerus as might have been known to Shelley, see *The Holy Bible, according to the Authorized Version with Notes, Explanatory and Practical*, 3 vols (London, 1839), ed. George D'Oyly and Richard Mant, vol. 1 (unpaginated), introduction to Book of Esther. For a summary of modern conjecture see *Encyclopaedia Judaica*, 16 vols (Jerusalem, 1971), entries on 'Ahasuerus' and 'Ahasuerus-Xerxes'. I am grateful to my colleague Dr T. J. Winnifrith for alerting me to the impossibility of making a positive identification of Ahasuerus with Xerxes: another possible candidate is Artaxerxes – according to D'Oyly and Mant, 'Artaxerxes Longimanus'. They also mention the opinion that Ahasuerus is 'Darius', presumably the Great, who also, of course, appears in *The Persae* – as a ghost. But Xerxes is certainly a strong candidate as well.

intertextual references. Shelley's Ahasuerus thus comprises the opposites of master and slave: as a Jew, given the name of a Persian ruler of
the Jews who, in the Book of Esther turns out to be a fairly enlightened
despot; and as one who has perhaps *been* Xerxes (what has Ahasuerus
not been?) offering advice to one who is, in effect, a second Xerxes.[19]
Ahasuerus contains the whole history of the world hitherto: he has
been master; he has been slave; and now, escaping from these hateful
contraries, he possesses that affinity with process, with the dissemina-
tions of self-delighting thought, which is the only hope of achieving
another Hellas.

---

[19] My thoughts are parallel with Jerome T. McGann's on 'poetic counterstate-
ment' in 'The Secrets of an Elder Day: Shelley after *Hellas*', *Keats-Shelley
Journal*, 15 (1966), p. 26.

Repetition's Music: The Triumph of Life

BERNARD BEATTY

A friend and colleague, hearing that I was engaged in an article on *The Triumph of Life* commented 'Shelley seems to say something once and then he says it again. Why does he do that?' The question, to which I had no very cogent answer, is a pertinent one. I will use it here as a way of keeping focus on the elusive doublings of Shelley's last text.

It is not as though answers to this question are hard to come by. We could say that *The Triumph of Life* is both more and less of an allegory that *The Divine Comedy*. It is beyond allegory because Shelley is seeking answers or insights through the begetting of images beyond his powers of rational articulation. On the other hand, unlike Dante, Shelley does not really expect to find or show anything that he does not already know. The poem therefore can only express this constituent incompatibility. It is held to the despair of its always terminated hope in a manner that cannot itself terminate. The sunrise which opens the poem is a simulacrum of all the openings of Life and Art. We experience it with exhilaration, then neutrality, distaste, and horror. We can mark this sequence, especially on re-reading, in 'inconsumably' (13), 'succession due' (15), 'mortal mould' (17), 'toil . . . imposed' (19–20). This sequence is repeatable because it is constitutive. It is horrifying because it produces deforming change out of seamless continuity. 'Inconsumably' turns into 'toil . . . imposed'. This is the type of all sequences in the poem for at no point can we see why or exactly how the change process goes wrong. The questions provoked by this inexplicable progression can only be answered by re-running the sequence until we tire. The 'we' is no slip of the pen, for we find ourselves represented inside-outside and then inside-inside its boundaries by the narrator. Like us, he is apparently wakeful and thus privileged outside the cycle of repetition which dawn inaugurates. In fact, this wakefulness serves only to bring Rousseau into view. He is the narrator's, but also our own, *semblable* who, grasping us as *frère*, tells us that we too will turn from spectator to 'Actor or victim in this wretchedness' (305). If, as we always will, we ask why this should be so, we can only be given another sequence in which the feet of the 'shape all light', delightful one moment will, in the next or same,

99

trample the fires of Rousseau's, or any reader's, mind 'into the dust of death' (388). Hence repetition is built into the poem.

Another starting point will reach the same conclusion. *The Divine Comedy* spirals its way through difference and ends up elsewhere than its starting place. The traditional apocalypse, on the other hand, unfolds within a frozen, unearthly moment the last rushes of time. The last book of the Bible for instance, is usually now read as though its apparently sequential images of destruction are repetitions of a single event.[1] Movement forwards is only apparent. Shelley's last poem does not have the journey character of Dante's vision and is, in some measure, an apocalypse even though amongst its array of various forms of light, it specifically does not have a vertical dimension in which to place the horizontal happenings of earthly history.[2] The 'sacred few' have 'Fled back like eagles to their native noon' (131) but the poet does not strain after them as he does in 'To a Sky-Lark' or the last lines of *Adonais*. Nevertheless this similarity with apocalyptic writings may help to furnish a generic answer to our question. It need not surprise us that the 'new vision' which bursts on Rousseau (410, 434) is a repetition for him of the 'shape all light' and, for us, a repetition of what the

---

1   Bernard McGinn in 'Revelation' in *The Literary Guide to the Bible*, eds. R. Alter and Frank Kermode (Collins, London, 1987. I quote from the paperback edition, Fontana, 1989) repeats the view of 'most modern scholars' that *Revelation* is 'a cyclical presentation of visions repeating or recapitulating the same basic message' (p. 525). For a summary of recent opinion and a bibliography see Adela Yarbro Collins, 'The Apocalypse' in *The New Jerome Biblical Commentary*, eds. R. E. Brown, J. A. Fitzmyer, R. E. Murphy (Prentice Hall, New Jersey, 1989; paperback edition Geoffrey Chapman 1991) 996–1016. We can put alongside McGinn's comment on *The Apocalypse*, G. M. Matthews's comment on *The Triumph* 'the body of the poem consists of two parallel accounts of the same experience', 'On Shelley's "The Triumph of Life" ', 106 (*Studia Neophilologica* Vol. xxxiv, 1962, 104–134). Matthews gives his own explanation for this phenomenon.
2   Shelley's comment in 'A Defence of Poetry' on 'the astonishing poetry of Moses, Job, David, Solomon, and Isaiah' is well known (*Shelley's Prose*, ed. D. L. Clark, Univ. of New Mexico Press, Albuquerque, 1954, corrected edit. 1966, 287). Though he invokes the model of prophecy in 'A Defence', 'Ode to the West Wind', and elsewhere, his own writing more frequently resembles apocalyptic. R. G. Woodman's *The Apocalyptic Vision in the Poetry of Shelley* (Univ. Toronto Press, 1964) is ostensibly concerned with this but the focus on 'apocalyptic' is imprecise. Brian Nellist has two judicious pages (167–168) on horizontal and vertical axes in Shelley's poetry in his remarkable article 'Shelley's Narratives and *The Witch of Atlas*' in *Essays on Shelley*, ed. Miriam Allott (Liverpool University Press, 1982) 160–190.

narrator has seen at the beginning of his 'trance of wondrous thought' (41).

Finally, alongside Dante, and John on Patmos, we could invoke Rousseau himself. In his *Confessions*, *Les Rêveries*, and even *La Nouvelle Héloise*, Rousseau dissolves the boundaries between fact and fiction, object and perception. He is an appropriately modern replacement for Dante's Vergil because the balance between the external condition and moral interior of the *Commedia's* inhabitants on the one hand, and the developing perception and moral growth of Dante in his progress past them is overturned in Shelley's vision by the interlocking subjectivities of Rousseau, narrator, and reader. Thus, as Timothy Clarke points out, the poem does not give the 'object of any genuine vision' but 'changed structures of perception'. Shelley makes this clear, Clarke argues, by his use of imagery to suggest 'the lingering of one state of consciousness as a possibility within that which succeeds it'.[3]

Hence again, any movement forward in the poem can only turn into a repeated discovery of the priority of perception's movement over that which it brings into view. What force then remains in our guiding question? It still seems unanswered. The ease with which answers can be found should be a warning in itself. The poem is facile and fluent. That is its difficulty. The tercets cannot be interrupted or turned back. Shelley knows exactly how to use them in order to excite and maintain a linear attentiveness. We anticipate whilst reading, a further clarity to which the cross-references already brought to our attention and held in the memory will be referred but, in the act of questioning, the poem maddeningly fades away. Instead of deterring us, this provokes us to reading on or reading again.

The best recent accounts of the poem, knowing this, are prepared to be perplexed and point to the perplexities inherent in Shelley's poetry without this being a reflex deconstructing gesture to language's indeterminacy. The recent studies by Michael O'Neill and Timothy Clarke,[4] in particular, have teased out the interrelation between the definite development of Shelley's thought and the deliberately less definite articulations of his verse with authority and tact. Richard Cronin similarly, quoted with approval by O'Neill, comments on *The*

---

[3] T. Clarke, *Embodying Revolution: the figure of the poet in Shelley* (Clarendon Press, Oxford, 1989).
[4] M. O'Neill, *The human mind's imagining's: conflict and achievement in Shelley's poetry* (Clarendon Press, Oxford, 1989).

Triumph that its 'value as a poem depends very much on how far its reader is prepared to accept and be satisfied with its labyrinthine inconclusiveness'.[5] Any proper reading of Shelley's best poetry must recognise in O'Neill's fine phrase, 'the tussle between the wish to state and the desire to evoke'.[6]

Is it possible to get any further than this? To do so is to ask questions about Shelley's questions and thus reintroduce the possibility of an answer. At all times this is hard but it is particularly so now when the priority of questions over answers is axiomatic. A. C. Bradley, the major critic of his day, could write a clear article on *The Triumph* at the beginning of the century[7] in the presumption that the critical task was to answer questions. That is not how we see it. Nevertheless a question, even if addressed to and coming from an indeterminacy, has to be specific in form. The 'Life' in Shelley's chariot is as indeterminate as may be ('as one whom', 'o'er what seemed the head') but the narrator's questions are particular and weighted. Their weight comes from the weariness of the watcher. He is initially 'wakeful' (22) then 'aghast' (107), 'struck to the heart' (176), then 'sick' (298). His questions come out of this definite weariness. The mixture of agitation and stupor in them corresponds to the random energy and entrapped lassitude that the vision holds together. Rousseau, similarly, is 'weary'. He can with difficulty summon the energy to declare his tale:

'I will tell all . . .
                           but I
Am weary' . . . Then like one who with the weight

Of his own words is staggered, wearily
              He paused, and ere he could resume, I cried,
'First who art thou?' . . .   (191, 195–199)

---

5   O'Neill, *The human mind's*, 175. R. Cronin notes the dissatisfaction felt even by admirers of the poem in his *Shelley's Poetic Thoughts* (Macmillan, Basingstoke, 1981) 222 and gives a list of these (259 no. 26).

6   O'Neill, *The human mind's*, 45.

7   A. C. Bradley, 'Notes on "The Triumph of Life" ', MLR (4, 1914) 441–456. Bradley answered in this article, for instance, the question why Plato was bound to the Car of Life. His explanation remains current. I am not in the smallest degree criticising Bradley. If we gave up thinking that questions could be answered, we would cease to pose them. Bradley had an article in the first issue of MLR (1, 1905) 25–42 'Notes on Passages in Shelley' which has two pages on *The Triumph*. He asserts, for example, that the charioteer in the car is Destiny rather than Time.

It will be evident that the narrator's question is activated here by his sense of the weight of what Rousseau knows.[8] Such weight is a form of knowledge that, at the same time, is linked with obliteration. The weight of understanding seems to crush understanding. Or, better, the weight *is* the understanding as, specifically, 'the heavy and the weary weight of all this unintelligible world'.[9] It is this moment of poise between articulation and obliteration that provokes the question 'I cried', much as a ghost is questioned more urgently at the moment of fading.[10] What the narrator does here, Rousseau has already done (though we hear of it later) when the 'shape all light' is suddenly seen to be engaged in obliterating 'the gazer's mind' and is about to wane herself:

> Ere she ceased
>
> To move, as one between desire and shame
> Suspended, I said – 'If, as it doth seem,
>   Thou comest from the realm without a name,
> Into this valley of perpetual dream,
>   Shew whence I came, and where I am, and why –
> Pass not away upon the passing stream.'   (393–399)

Rousseau's question, like the narrator's, is brought into being by suspended terror provoked equally by fear of what might be divulged and by fear that the speaker will fade before a full answer can be given. The intersecting point of these two lines of fear is the origin of existential questioning. Whether this is the right word for this poem must detain us a little.

To support the appropriateness of 'existential', we might look again at Rousseau's three questions and note that they form a single enquiry with three terms:

> Shew whence I came, and where I am, and why –

8 Other indications of Rousseau's weariness are at 334, 401, 430, 540–1.
9 'Lines composed . . . above Tintern Abbey' 39–40. William Wordsworth *The Poems*, ed. J. O. Hayden (Penguin, Harmondsworth, 1977) 358.
10 See, for instance, Manfred's frantic questioning of the fading Astarte in *Manfred II*, iv. There is a parallel of a kind in 'Julian and Maddalo' where the sunset is held onto as it disappears:
>   'ere it fade'
>   Said my Companion, 'I will shew you soon
>   A better station.'   85–87.

There are three such clusters of threefold questioning in the poem plus the final, single question 'Then, what is life?' These are at lines 177, 296, and 398. In addition the narrator, on first seeing the vision, uses a similar three-term formula:

> All hastening onward, yet none seemed to know
>   Whither he went or whence he came, or why   (46–47)

That three terms are important is shown by the elision of four terms back into three. For instance, when the narrator asks:

> 'Whence camest thou and whither goest thou?
> How did thy course begin', I said, 'and why'?   (296–297)

We notice that 'whence' and 'whither' are put together. In Rousseau's careful reply to this question the four terms are assembled differently:

> 'Whence I came, partly I seem to know,
>
> And how and by what paths I have been brought
>   To this dread pass, methinks even thou mayst guess;
> Why this should be my mind can compass not;
>
> Whither the conqueror hurries me still less.   (300–304)

Here 'why' and 'whither' are differentiated but put together because Rousseau does not know the answer to them. The effect, typical of the poem, is both of the interchangeability of the questions and of an effort being made to discriminate between them. 'Whence' and 'how' and 'what' are joined by indiscriminate copulas and the parallel formulas 'I seem to know' and 'thou mayst guess'. Both the diversification and singleness testify to weariness. Or, more precisely, in a hideous reversal of 'The One remains, the many change and pass', the poet now fuses and confuses together what *Adonais* finally manages to separate:

> Mine eyes are sick of this perpetual flow
> Of people, and my heart of one say thought. –   (298–299)

It does seem fair, on this inspection, to revive the word 'existential' for this single weariness to death which provokes an authentic question in the face of a multiplied inauthenticity of lives. Such weariness (we could as well call it 'angst', 'sorge', 'fret') *is* the authenticity. It is why my colleague was right to remember *The Triumph* in terms of a repetition and an insoluble question which summoned the poem back to him. Some corroboration of this emphasis can be found in St Augustine whose proto-existentialist *Confessions* were used for the epigraph to *Alastor*: 'Nondum amabam, et amare amabam, quaerebam quid amarem, amans amore' ('Not yet did I love, yet I was in love with loving; . . . I sought what I might love, loving to love').[11] The quotation would fit the author of Rousseau's *Confessions* just as well. It is unlikely that Shelley would approve this quotation from St Augustine's *City of God* (xi, 21)

> But there are three things above all which we need to know about a created thing, three things which we should be told: who made it, how he made it, and why he made it. That is why the scripture says, 'God said: "Let there be Light": and light was created. And God saw that the light was good'. So the answer to our question 'Who?' is 'God'. To the question 'How?' the answer is, 'He said: "Let it be"; and it was created.' And to 'Why?' we get the reply, 'It was good.'[12]

The author of *Queen Mab* would doubtless have made Voltairean and somewhat prissy fun out of this magisterial supplying of answers to a threefold questioning. Voltaire, however, is one of life's captives and Rousseau himself is foregrounded so as to problematize the modernity he represents. Rousseau, it seems, epitomises the transition from sensibility as a sign of aristocratic breeding to its new role transforming burghers into men of feeling who are to become introspective, poetic, and in harmony with their natural surroundings. He is thus a foretaste of the potentialities of civilisation. On the other hand, that proneness to frailty and decay, which so marks the beautiful poet figures of Shelley's verse from the beginning, becomes in the 'cripple' Rousseau a

---

[11] St Augustine, *Confessions* 111, i. The translation is that given in Reiman, *Shelley*, 70.

[12] St Augustine, *The City of God*, trans. H. Bettenson (Penguin, Harmondsworth, 1972) 452–3.

Quia vero tria quaedam maxime scienda de creatura nobis oportuit intimari, quis eam fecerit, per quid fecerit, quare fecerit: *Dixit Deus*, inquit: Fiat lux, et facta est lux. Et vidit Deus lucem quia bona est. Si ergo quaerimus, quis fecerit: *Deus est*; si per quid fecerit: *Dixit: Fiat et facta est*; si quare fecerit: *quia bona est*.

De. Civ. Dei, (Lipsiae, 1877–1892 2 vols.), 1, xi, 21 (p. 489).

ghastly indictment of that prized potentiality which, even now, he has not surrendered. Such interractions of decay and infinite desire are closer to Augustine than to Voltaire. Certainly the threefold questions which punctuate the poem are strikingly similar to Augustine's. Like Augustine, too, the interrogation is of the nature of light (Sun, star-light, glare, 'shape all light', 'true Sun'). Beyond light, so to speak, is a disbelieving question about the God who makes things 'irreconcilable' (230). Within light, so to speak, is a desperate question about ageing and, maybe, Jane Williams.[13] The questioning is from a disappearing substance to a disappearing substance within a light (of existence and of intelligibility) which has neither stability nor trustworthiness. The last question of the poem 'Then, what is Life?' is not a request for more information – we already know that Life is a deformed form that deforms – but a cry like that which sets Christian running at the opening of the *The Pilgrim's Progress*. But running, here, circles the car of Life.

The most important word in the last question of the poem is 'Then'. It seems real. Whatever there is left to inaugurate or conclude in 'Happy those for whom the fold of' (547), the poem cannot now give us any more repetitions. We have reached this point: 'given that life is this, then, what is life?' It betokens exactly the same mixture of recognition of limits and insistence on something further that con-stitutes Rousseau's weariness. The narrator is become, as Rousseau prophesied, 'Actor or victim in this wretchedness' (305). He is the wedding guest become mariner and held to the repetition of someone else's sequence as his own. Coleridge conceals the emptiness of this assimilation by cheering us up with a naive moral. Shelley prevents us from, even *en passant*, imagining that we or the narrator are sadder and wiser. The difference is in the reiterated question. The point we have reached is more like that of the last word of Byron's Cain:

CAIN.   Oh Abel!
ADAM.   Peace be with him.
CAIN.   But with *me*![14]

[13] This remains probable even if G. M. Matthews's specific claims about Jane Williams's connections with the poem are not accepted. See G. M. Matthews 'The Triumph of Life'.
[14] *Lord Byron's Cain*, ed. T. G. Steffan (Univ. Texas Press, Austin, 1968) 258.

The reference to Byron will help us because 'his' central declaration in *Julian and Maddalo* seems analogous to that of Rousseau:

> 'And such,' – he cried, 'is our mortality
> And this must be the emblem and the sign
> Of what should be eternal and divine! –
> And like that black and dreary bell, the soul,
> Hung in a heaven-illumined tower, must toll
> Our thoughts and our desires to meet below
> Round the rent heart and pray – as madmen do
> For what? they know not, – till the night of death
> As sunset that strange vision, severeth
> Our memory from itself, and us from all
> We sought and yet were baffled!' (120–130)

With wonderful delicacy, Shelley claims that this speech is faithful to Maddalo's sense but mars 'The force of his expressions' (131). Certainly, the word 'baffled' is one that Byron often uses[15] and Shelley does not. Would it be the right word for that last question 'Then, what is Life?' Maddalo, in a parallel formula, asserts rather than questions: ' "And such," – he cried, "is our mortality".' This assertion is made up of a confident diagnosis which terminates in bafflement and bitter prayer. It invites assent. Moreover, though the diagnosis is of mutability and is itself bound up with the sunset which is agent and sign of this mutability, yet Maddalo's cry has memorable definition over and above the conditions set out as obliterating that definition. Maddalo knows this himself. This is, after all, how *Childe Harold* is written. It is not Shelley's method. In *Julian and Maddelo*, he sets Maddalo's assertion of 'is' and 'must be' over against Julian's insistence on potentiality. In between, as exemplum, is the maniac who is a nicer version of Shelley's Rousseau. The poem ends, significantly in a flurry of questions:

> 'She left him' . . . 'Why, her heart must have been tough:
> How did it end?' 'And was not this enough?
> They met – they parted' – 'Child, is there no more?'

---

[15] Shelley uses 'baffles' twelve times in his poetry. None of the usages is important. Byron uses it over forty times, many times significantly. In *Manfred* alone, for instance, there are four 'baffled' and one 'baffle'. For a random parallel, we could note that 'silence' is used almost exactly the same number of times by both poets.

> 'Something within that interval which bore
> The stamp of *why* they parted, *how* they met:'
> . . .
> I urged and questioned still, she told me how
> All happened – but the cold world shall not know.
>   (606–610, 616–617)

There is in these last lines that characteristic sense of something coyly proffered and withheld which is present in the deliberated last lines of *The Witch of Atlas*.

> I will declare another time; for it is
> A tale more fit for the weird winter nights
> Than for these garish summer days, when we
> Scarcely believe much more than we can see.   (669–672)

If Shelley is baffled here, he is careful not to seem so. The conversational structure of *Julian and Maddalo*, incomplete as it is, and the serious whimsy of *The Witch of Atlas* constitute the art without which nothing would be said or shown by this poet. From this perspective, Maddalo's declaration, which does not hide his bafflement, is crude. It would deflect us, despite its rhetorical shaping, out of art and into the bitterness of Life or into prayer arising out of that bitterness. Nevertheless, by acknowledging, placing, and thus refusing to be it, Shelley is able to come much closer to Maddalo's position in the poem than he could otherwise allow himself to do. Similarly, in *The Witch of Atlas*, he can articulate a disgust identical to that of *The Triumph*,

> while they were still arraying
> In liveries ever new, the rapid, blind
> And fleeting generations of mankind.   (613–616)

precisely because the stanza, thus concluded, privileges a counter-image of the body 'warm and undecaying' (610). The two images are in equipoise like Julian and Maddalo themselves.

What then of that final question in *The Triumph?* It is clear that Rousseau and the narrator are not in balancing equipoise. Indeed the poem begins with that image of Dawn which, even when one knows from repeated reading that it is going to be discredited, always retains its power as a positive image, however provisional, in its own right. It can neither exist as an indisputable counter to the glare of the car of light nor be read wholly ironically. At least, this is true of the reader who reads as opposed to the reader whose reflection is founded on purposeful cross-reference. This distinction, so dangerous to insist upon, is brought into play again and again by Shelley. Maddalo, so to say, temporarily gathers up the whole of himself into his ' "And such", he cried, "is our mortality" ', just as Byron in *Childe Harold* does in such lines as 'Our life is a false nature' or 'There is a very life in our despair'.[16] Shelley avoids this manifest disclosure of voice except in his lyrics. Even there we know that his lyrics are often intended dramatically[17] and that lyrical 'I's can never be straightforward. Nevertheless, the final group of lyrics concerned with Jane Williams are as personally directed as any group of poems can be. It is only with difficulty (though of course it can still be done) that we can, in our usual professional way, still talk of a speaker when the poet concludes 'To Jane: The Recollection' with these lines:

> Less oft is peace in S[helley]'s mind
> Than calm in water seen.[18]

It will be granted, perhaps by all, that 'S . . .'s mind' is and is not 'Shelley's mind' which is and is not Shelley's mind. 'Lines written in the Bay of Lerici' was 'drafted on two conjugate leaves of the paper on which Shelley wrote *The Triumph of Life*'.[19] It would be odd if there was no relation at all, of mood and emotional origin, between these remarkable lyrics and *The Triumph*. Shelley's poetry, to be sure, is full of surprising distances. His ability to change mode and maintain the peculiar timbre of his major productions is striking. His verse is more and more adroit at using, but also keeping at bay, the pressure of Shelley's strong sensibility and articulated opinions. Apart from his dramas, he comes increasingly to share the knowledge of this adroitness with his readers. In the case of *The Witch of Atlas*, this becomes the content as well as the manner of the poem. Nevertheless *The Triumph of Life*, the cleverest and most audacious of Shelley's poems, is perilously close to exposing this adroitness as bankruptcy, and thus to exposing Shelley himself. It lives out of this risk. I mean by this that Shelley allows the weariness which cuts off the poet's flight in *Epipsy-*

---

16 *Childe Harold's Pilgrimage* IV, 136; III, 34.
17 See G. M. Matthews 'Shelley's lyrics' in *The Morality of Art*, ed. D. W. Jefferson (London, 1969) 195–209.
18 'The Recollection', 86–87. Printed as in Reiman, *Shelley's Poetry*, 446.
19 Reiman, *Shelley's Poetry*, 452 n. 5.

chilion and reverses the entire drift of *Hellas* in its very last stanza, into the whole of his last poem. However elaborately structured it is therefore, and however brilliantly it assimilates Ezekiel, Dante, Petrarch, and Rousseau, it voices a single, lyric weariness. The tripartite questions which inaugurate its giant sections function in a similar way to the repeated formulas initiating stanzas in Shelley's lyrics[20] or to the rhetorically signposted sections of 'Ode to the West Wind'. The device which should prevent this from happening (Rousseau as the narrator's interlocutor) is the very other who turns out to be the narrator's doppelganger. Unlike Dante therefore, who ascends and leaves Vergil behind because the Life that moves him and the Universe takes him in a single movement to three circles and a single light beyond questioning, the narrator ends up stuck with Rousseau and a frozen question. That is why the 'wonder' worthy of Dante's rhyme (471) is so surreal a parody of love's transforming power and why, as J. J. McGann noted,[21] the word 'transfigured' (475) is used blasphemously to mean disfigured.

How can weariness answer a question? This must be our final concentration. Through it, perhaps, we may be able both to justify the repetitions of the poem and decide whether its questioning is existential. Logically, a question involves more than one. The questioning self, too, seeks another or divides itself into two. Answering, on the other hand, dissolves this duality into one. Answers necessarily include the question they answer now obliterated as a question. Dante's questioning of Vergil is normally like this. Similarly, in *The Triumph* when the narrator asks

'Who is he with chin
Upon his breast and hands crost on his chain?'   (216–217)

and Rousseau tells him that it is Napoleon, the question has ceased to exist because a single recognition is now common. When, however, the narrator cries out 'Then, what is Life?' the 'then' calls attention to an already existing assimilation of question and answer. It is already answered by the now interchangeable experience of Rousseau and the speaker.

We could call this a lyrical question and answer rather than a

---

[20] For instance the last four stanzas of 'Rarely, rarely comest thou' and the first three stanzas of 'Sleep, sleep on! forget thy pain'.
[21] J. J. McGann 'The Secrets of an Elder Day: Shelley after Hellas', 268 in *Shelley*, ed. R. B. Woodings (Macmillan, London, 1968) 253–271.

logical or discursive one. Broadly speaking, this is the method of Wordsworth's lyrical ballads. These explain usually in answer to a question, by a mixture of symbol and narrative, why the speaker is thus and lead us to moral insight by enlarging our sympathy. In Shelley's more 'mystical' lyrical ballad,[22] the originating question neither is nor becomes anchored in Wordsworth's manner. The speaker is definitely somewhere but only by courtesy of dawn, symbolic detail, and a 'trance'. The 'somewhere' is shifting and untrustworthy. The speaker's cry announces this fact just as Rousseau questions the 'shape all light' at the moment when her presence and her fading are horribly combined. By the 'end' of the poem, the reader also consciously shares the same shifting ground as Rousseau and narrator. Hence the narrator's question is no longer a question because there is no other to put it to. My own experience of reading the poem many times is that, bit by bit, I have ceased to interrogate it. Questions are impossible from an experience which sees itself as circular and terminated. This is exactly the opposite pole in Shelley's verse from, for example, D. J. Hughes's statement that in Act IV of *Prometheus Unbound* 'Potentiality indeed exceeds every existentiality'. Hughes talks of this as 'an apocalyptic stasis'.[23] Two kinds of 'apocalyptic stasis' may be sketched out and they correspond to two forms of lyrical recognition. The first is Being as Coming-into-Being ('Life of Life!' 'Child of Light!'), the other is Being as Deformation ('the rapid, blind and fleeting generations of mankind'). The discursive underpinning of the first three acts of *Prometheus Unbound* and of Rousseau's answers to the narrator's questions are always destined to be subsumed into pure lyric weightlessness and weight respectively.

It begins to look as though 'existential' is not the right word after all. But in thus severing the poem from that ancestry (Lucretius, Augustine, Dante) which appears to guarantee the equipoise of discourse and lyricism, have we turned the poem into an extended version of Schumann's 'Warum?'? This well-known piano piece depends upon the wistful repetition of an arrested, upward cadence. The piece's aesthetic charm nullifies the purported existential unrest of its question-mark. We recall perhaps, Shelley's maniac 'sitting mournfully

---

[22] 'One of the most mystical of his poems, the *Triumph of Life*' (Mary Shelley). *The Complete Poetical Works of Percy Byshe Shelley* (Oxford Standard Authors, London, 1935) 669.

[23] D. J. Hughes, 'Potentiality in Prometheus Unbound', 159 in *Shelley*, ed. Woodings, 142–161.

Near a piano' in 'an apartment opening on the sea' (271–3). He is not, in fact, an example of Maddalo's dictum:

> Most wretched men
> Are cradled into poetry by wrong,
> They learn in suffering what they teach in song.   (543–546)

Unlike Margaret in Wordworth's 'A Ruined Cottage', Shelley's madman is a lesser figure than those who talk about him. Rousseau, more substantial than his interlocutor, has learnt nothing from his suffering. The narrator, like Rousseau and maniac, has nothing to 'teach in song' beyond the enacted weariness of his lyric question.

The Triumph of Life is, indeed, shockingly close to the aesthetic of much nineteenth-century music by such composers as Berlioz, Schumann, Chopin, Liszt, and Tchaikovsky. Like so much of that music, its aesthetic cross-referencing of great literary and historical themes from the Greeks, the Bible, Dante, Petrarch, Rousseau, Goethe, Byron, in lengthy, apparently purposive, but repetitive structures based on leitmotifs representing the trapped but still asserting self, is offered as an equivalent to salvation. Julian, listening to the madman's music and seeing its effects on the disordered sensibilities around him, opines:

> Methinks there were
> A cure of these with patience and kind care,
> If music can thus move . . . (288–230)

If this is so, then my friend's question about repetitions can be returned to him. He is guilty of a category mistake. It is the nature of music to say it all again. Shelley's lyrics depend upon repetition for their music. The repetition may reveal desperation but, aesthetically, it is therapeutic. The opening declaration by the narrator tells us that he recognised 'the freshness of that dawn' as a repetition of a past sameness so that the tenses already in the past ('was') are pushed a notch further back ('I had felt'). We will always be anxiously disposed to grasp as much intellectual meaning and bare circumstance as we can when we set out to read the poem with this indication. But Donald Tovey would, in my view, read it better than Donald Reiman.[24] That is to say,

---

[24] Donald Tovey's magnificent Essays in Musical Analysis (1935–9) are still in print. The accident of a common first name is partly responsible for the pairing

these lines are not primarily signalling us towards the intellectual meaning that our knowledge and our being are given to us as fading repetitions but that the poem's life will consist of this repeated discovery. We should set out to read the poem expecting the echo of this haunting sameness in all its unfolded difference. In the phrase 'I knew That I had felt' (33–34) the 'knew' and the 'felt' lose themselves in 'that' and 'had'. St Augustine's intellectual push to a ground beyond his questions' scope which ensures the possibility of answering is here beside the point. 'That' and 'had' are a modality in themselves. The 'I had felt' here in the poem's first few bars is already the 'Then, what is Life?' of its unconcluded conclusion. New visions are old visions. We will tire of this meaning and of the pursuit of meaning but not of this tiredness itself which remains as a fresh cadence gathering expressive force in the music of the poem. *The Triumph* is the most mannered and the most authentic of Shelley's poems. He finds in it a way to solve his problems with the art of long poems by confessing more directly to the weariness which is normally the unallowed contrary to the energies of the West Wind, or to the weightlessly active Witch of Atlas. This weariness, innately lyrical, now founds rather than confounds his purported structures and yet seems to represent something comparably serious to Dante's writings. Most lyric poems, in most languages, put together in various ways a 'freshness' and a 'had'. That is all they do, though 'know' and 'feel' linger in attendance. *The Triumph of Life* does exactly this and triumphs as art in consequence. Yet, in comparison with Dante (and Shelley invites the comparison), there is something shocking about this. There is no intellectual way through the poem. Any pattern that presents itself turns out to be provisional and inconsistent. We feel no sympathy of any kind for Rousseau, for the 'mighty captives' or for the 'ribald crowd' whereas Dante's trapped, purgatorial, or blissful persons are registered over and above what they signify. We are directed in *The Triumph of Life* by a very intelligent man, using his intelligence, to his final, fully accomplished and aesthetically stilled, version of the horror stories that Shelley compulsively read to the impressionable in order to share the impersonal terror generated in

with Donald Reiman. It remains appropriate because Reiman's reading is, in my view, too earnestly contextual to be a reading. All readers of the poem are, of course, deeply indebted to Reiman's energy, acumen, and judgement as scholar and editor.

them.[25] The accomplishment here, as with Yeats, seems consciously bound up with a fashioning coldness. Shelley, so far as we can tell, had some intimation of this and was appalled by it. Something of this, it is hard to say exactly how, communicates itself in and through the reflexive art of the poem. This is why it is both mannered and authentic.

It is for this reason too, that the best critical reading of *The Triumph of Life* remains that of Paul de Man.[26] In other hands the referring back of Rousseau's disfigurement to the intrinsic disfiguring of the figured (language) would be a purely intellectual sollicitation to current controversies. But De Man communicates the real horror of this with something of Shelley's own exactness and zest. The disallowed word 'Life' which, as we know only too well, is merely one fading figure within Shelley's music, seems in De Man's essay as in Shelley's poem to echo as a question that is real and uncontained.

---

[25] This is well brought out in R. Holmes, *Shelley The Pursuit* (Quartet Books, London, 1974) 113–114, 259–262.
[26] Paul de Man, *The Rhetoric of Romanticism* (Columbia University Press, New York, 1984).

'And all things seem only one':
the Shelleyan Lyric

MICHAEL O'NEILL

1

'It is only when under the overruling influence of some one state of
feeling, either actually experienced, or summoned up in almost the
vividness of reality by a fervid imagination, that he writes as a great
poet'.[1] J. S. Mill's observation about Shelley, which he thought held
particularly true of the poet's 'lyrical poems',[2] may seem to be borne
out by the 'fervid' intensity of poems such as 'O World, O Life, O
Time' or 'The Flower That Smiles Today'. But in both these late pieces
the poet's 'labour of simplification'[3] does not exclude complication or
nuance. In the latter poem image and abstraction combine sugges-
tively, inviting speculation about experiences to which its mood might
apply: failure in personal relations, the collapse of political ideals, and
metaphysical scepticism are all candidates.[4] Moreover, Shelley
ironically contravenes generic expectations. These stem from the
lyric's emphasis on transience, which appears, misleadingly, to herald
advice to 'Gather ye Rose-buds while ye may'. If the opening lines,
'The flower that smiles today / Tomorrow dies' (ll. 1–2),[5] are an abbre-
viating lift from the just-quoted poem by Herrick ('And this same

---

[1] J. S. Mill, 'Two Kinds of Poetry' (1833), quoted from *Shelley: Shorter Poems
and Lyrics*, A Casebook, ed. Patrick Swinden (London and Basingstoke, 1976),
p. 58; hereafter Casebook.
[2] 'Two Kinds of Poetry', quoted from Casebook, p. 58.
[3] The phrase is T. S. Eliot's in his 'William Blake', *Selected Essays*, 3rd
enlarged edn (1951; London, 1976), p. 317.
[4] G. M. Matthews argues that 'the poem was evidently written for the opening of *Hellas*', in 'Shelley's Lyrics' (1969), quoted from Casebook, p. 189.
Judith Chernaik, however, in *The Lyrics of Shelley* (Cleveland and London,
1972), hereafter Chernaik, argues that 'the lyric appears to be self-sufficient'
(p. 161), a view I share.
[5] Quoted from *Shelley's Poetry and Prose*, Norton Critical Edition, ed. Donald
H. Reiman and Sharon B. Powers (New York and London, 1977); hereafter
PP. All poems by Shelley are quoted from this edition, unless otherwise indicated.

flower that smiles to day, / To morrow will be dying'),[6] there is, from
the start of Shelley's lyric, a tight-lipped acquiescence in the intoler-
able quite at odds with the seventeenth-century poem's acceptance of
the inevitable. 'All that we wish to stay / Tempts and then flies' (ll.
3–4), Shelley asserts, his verbs tracing a circuit of monosyllabic disap-
pointment. 'This world's delight' may be 'Brief even as bright' (ll. 5, 7).
Yet the injunction to enjoy the present which ghosts line 7 never
materializes, giving way to the statement that some things do last,
though in altered form: virtue, friendship and love 'Survive their joy,
and all / Which ours we call' (ll. 13–14).

These lines show Shelley's ability to embed astute insights in a
seemingly traditional idiom. Here it is the writing's elliptical compact-
ness which puts its lyric idiom under pressure, and implies the persistence in shrunken form of betrayed ideals that expose to us our
alienation from what we thought 'ours'. In the last stanza the use of
'Whilst' (ll. 15, 17 and 19) hints that the lyric will be rounded off by a
Romantic equivalent to 'seize the day'. Sardonically, though, the en-
suing imperative, 'Dream thou' (l. 20), denies the possibility of anything but illusion as an alternative or prelude to the disillusionment
tersely expressed by the last line, 'Then wake to weep' (l. 21). There,
the lachrymose is held in check by a bitterness which the final rhyme
clinches (each stanza ends with a triplet). Such bitterness bespeaks the
achieved presence of a lyric voice in a poem that avoids the word 'I'.

On the face of it 'O World, O Life, O Time' is a quintessentially
Romantic lyric complaint; the poem uses its refrain and repeated
rhyme to underscore 'one state of feeling', a Shelleyan version of
Wordsworthian loss.[7] Yet without losing the air of being directed by
some 'overruling influence' the poem prompts thought about the exact
nature of that influence, an influence suggested by the 'peculiar compression'[8] of the opening:

> O World, O Life, O Time,
> On whose last steps I climb,
> Trembling at that where I had stood before . . . (ll. 1–3)

---

6 'To the Virgins, to Make Much of Time', quoted from *The Poems of Robert
Herrick* (London, New York, Toronto and Melbourne, 1902). On 'Shelley's
version of carpe diem' see Chernaik, p. 155.
7 Poem is quoted from text in Chernaik, p. 246. For the influence of
Wordsworth's 'Ode: Intimations of Immortality' see Chernaik, pp. 146–7.
8 Chernaik, p. 147.

The reader is struck here less by 'the bonding of the literal and meta-phorical'[9] than by the way potent feeling subordinates any logic of metaphor to its own demands; the lines freeze the poet in a posture of endless climbing of 'last steps' on which he 'had stood before'. Shelley may pit the vulnerable lyric 'I' against the abstractions of 'World', 'Life' and 'Time', as though the self were overwhelmed by vast imper-sonal forces. Yet his question, 'When will return the glory of your prime?' (l. 4), projects onto world, life and time the sense of loss experienced by the 'I'. World, life and time, then, are both opposed to the self and words for the dimensions in and through which the self exists; indeed, the stanza half-suggests that the opening line's categories only exist by virtue of the poet's fall into awareness of loss. The second stanza undergoes tonal shifts without forfeiting the im-pression of conveying 'one state of feeling'. Apostrophe and question modulate into uncomprehending statement in the line, 'A joy has taken flight' (l. 7), a line which mutes the poem's tone (it is not 'joy' but 'A joy' which has fled) and is the more affecting for doing so. Again, the poem moves the reader by glancing at the fact that the poet himself has not lost the capacity to be moved; he can feel 'grief' but not 'delight' (l. 9), a discovery that combines lament and under-statement (there is no analysis of why this should be the case). The final line 'No more, O never more!' (l. 10) repeats the fifth line; but where that line was full of freshly located distress the later line is heavy with a sense of unalterable regret. The poem, then, aspires to the formal mastery which is lyric's seductive compensation for the dis-tresses of experience; at the same time the notion of the isolated lyric 'I' is explored as well as asserted.

Applied to these poems, as to others by Shelley, the judgement of J. S. Mill with which this essay began is stimulating yet vulnerable on a number of counts: it presupposes, in G. M. Matthews's sardonic phrasing, that 'the lyrical heart-cry is Shelley's typical utterance';[10] it ignores the fact that even lyrical heart-cries work within (or against) generic constraints; and it discounts Shelley's capacity to render com-plicated states of feeling within a single poem, indeed to redefine, albeit subtly rather than blatantly, the lyric form. Privileging 'some one state of feeling' as cause and effect of lyric, Mill's remark asks to be deconstructed. Tilottama Rajan does just this and yet more than this,

9 Chernaik, p. 147.
10 'Shelley's Lyrics', quoted from Casebook, p. 178.

arguing that the 'dismantling of lyric autotelism is something which happened in Romantic texts themselves'.[11] In a sense, Rajan is fighting a rearguard action against the devaluing of lyric implicit in the post-structuralist idiom she employs. Thus she contends that Romantic poets contrived an 'interdiscursive' form of lyric in the act of dismantling lyric's 'monological autonomy', and concludes that 'the survival of the lyrical voice testifes to an understanding of the self that is not quite that of poststructuralism'.[12]

Rajan's essay valuably qualifies pre-theoretical and post-structuralist assumptions. Yet Mill's emphasis on Shelley's evocations of 'some one state of feeling' is still salutary because it provokes thought about the degree of 'autonomy', 'monological' or otherwise, attained by Shelley's lyrics. Even so 'dialogic' a poem as 'The Two Spirits – An Allegory' offers us less a picture of the mind's debate with itself (such as is supplied by Keats's 'Ode to a Nightingale') than the interplay of two 'single states of feeling'. If each spirit sees because of what it is, the poem itself achieves a kind of 'monological autonomy' by dictating the terms through which the poem's clash of perspectives is mediated. So the last two stanzas may offer contrasting emblems of the outlooks of the two spirits, but it is the lyric poet who asserts a final control over his poem's voices, exhibiting the changes that can be rung on a single word, 'shape' (ll. 38 and 45).

Certainly many of Shelley's lyrics, in the interests of a singleness or unity desired though rarely attained, tend not to pause over or point up, even as they recognize, the complex, the unassimilable, the contradictory. Rajan defines 'autonomy' or 'lyric consciousness' as coming 'as close as possible' to 'a consciousness without the dimension of being-in-the-world'.[13] Shelley's lyrics never aspire unproblematically to 'autonomy' in this sense; but neither are they prepared simply to make lyric consciousness dependent on some contextualizing discourse. Their pursuit of autonomy is more a question of seeking to organize their figurative inventions into imaginative structures that give the impression, possibly the illusion, of being self-sustaining. In this sense the final section of 'Ode to the West Wind' achieves a precarious autonomy in the act of admitting the self's dependence both on the

---

[11] Tilottama Rajan, 'Romanticism and the Death of Lyric Consciousness', hereafter Rajan, in *Lyric Poetry: Beyond New Criticism*, ed. Chaviva Hošek and Patricia Parker (Ithaca and London, 1985), p. 198.

[12] Rajan, pp. 206, 196, 207.

[13] Rajan, p. 196.

wind for inspiration and on an audience, 'mankind', for actualizing the potential of the poet's 'words' (l. 67). Fiercely competing emotions are bound together by the onward impulsion of the terza rima. The section's initial desire that the speaker be granted the status of a natural object governed by the wind is expressed in words that deconstruct even as they formulate the desire. To be a lyre 'even as the forest is' (l. 57) is impossible given the presence of consciousness in the lyric 'I'; the next line ('What if my leaves are falling like its own!' (l. 58)), poignantly yet almost jokily, behaves as if the problem stemmed from the processes of change and decay to which the self, like the forest, is subject. But the problem lies more in the very existence of the self which the poem pleads that the wind will possess: 'Be thou me, impetuous one!' (l. 62). The plea for unity tacitly recognises its impossibility, passing into an assertion of the lyric self's mastery; it is 'by the incantation of this verse' (l. 65) that Shelley hopes his words will reach mankind. Ronald Tetreault lays emphasis on the poet's willingness at the end of 'Ode to the West Wind' 'not to force his meaning on his auditors but to yield them their autonomy'.[14] Yet it is important, too, to recognize the degree to which the poem resonates within the echo-chamber of its own figurative explorations: 'incantation', for instance, sends us back to, while reversing the implications of, the early simile of the leaves as 'ghosts from an enchanter fleeing' (l. 3).

2

Lyric autonomy, the sense that the poet's words have shaped themselves into a self-sufficient discourse, is only ever momentary in Shelley, an impression, a 'sense'; hence its pathos and unstable value. Nowhere in Shelley is its presence more intriguing than in *Prometheus Unbound*. In Rajan's view the lyrical drama foregrounds 'the tension between lyric and drama'. But though she asserts that '*Prometheus* is not so much an interiorizing of the dramatic form as an exteriorizing of the lyrical',[15] it is equally arguable that, at key moments in the work, lyric converts drama into its own substance. So the 'Life of Life' lyric (II. v. 48–71) not only brings to a climax the second act's imagining of

---

[14] Ronald Tetreault, *The Poetry of Life: Shelley and Literary Form* (Toronto, Buffalo and London, 1987), p. 220; hereafter Tetreault.
[15] Rajan, pp. 204, 202.

change, but also marks the moment at which the second act actualizes its promise of vision; temporarily, the lyrical drama resolves into 'one state of feeling', albeit a state compounded out of different states.

'Life of Life!': the exclamation is both creative of its subject and beyond the scope of philosophical or mythological translation. Life is breathed into 'life' by a use of words that communicates awareness of inadequacy and wonder. The rhythm is incantatory yet ordered, 'life' setting up alliterative intimacies with 'lips' and 'love' that begin a bewildering celebration of the division between and inseparability of spirit and body, love and life, essence and appearance, ideal and projection. No other terms will suffice, the wording of 'Life of Life!' implies, and yet the second and fourth stanzas begin with phrases ('Child of Light!' (l. 54) and 'Lamp of Earth!' (l. 66)) which both build on the implications of the opening and intimate the possibility of innumerable fresh starts to the poem.

The transfigured Asia is known only as she is being defined in a lyric that is concerned with the impossibility of definition. Crucial to the poem's effectiveness, however, is the sureness with which 'impossibility of definition' is conveyed. Stephen Spender commented on the 'confused machinery' of the opening stanza's imagery, asking, in relation to lines 51–3 ('then screen them / In those looks, where whoso gazes / Faints, entangled in their mazes'), 'How can you be screened by looks which are also mazes in which whoever gazes becomes entangled and faints?'[16] One answer is Bloom's: 'Shelley is not sending [us] to the sketching board.'[17] This is true, but Bloom does not acknowledge the degree to which Shelley negotiates with, even as he departs from, the prospect of visualization. The word order of lines 51–3 persuades the reader to trust in a series of telescoped suggestions. 'Screen' benefits from a syntax flexible enough to permit two possible and, in reading, overlapping subjects:[18] 'lips' (l. 48), in which case it is the movement of the lips that changes the face from 'smiles' to entangling looks, or the 'smiles' (l. 50) themselves, in which case the 'smiles' veil themselves – as though residually abiding – behind the 'looks'.

16 Stephen Spender, *Shelley* (1952), quoted from *Shelley's 'Prometheus Unbound': A Variorum Edition*, ed. Lawrence John Zillman (Seattle, 1959), p. 491.
17 Harold Bloom, *Shelley's Mythmaking* (1959; Ithaca, NY, 1969), p. 126; hereafter Bloom.
18 Isobel Armstrong writes perceptively about the work performed by Shelley's 'ambiguous syntax' in the poem in her *Language as Living Form in Nineteenth-Century Poetry* (Sussex and New Jersey, 1982), p. 137; hereafter Armstrong.

On either interpretation, the language proposes that the 'thou' manifests itself through appearances that are and are not identical with the essence they conceal and reveal. The 'looks' are '*those* looks' (my emphasis), where Shelley's avoidance of a duff epithet propels the reader forward; the looks are those 'where whoso gazes / Faints'; the metre's stress on 'Faints' puts sinew into potentially weak writing, forcing together action and consequence (gazing and fainting). It is at this point of possible arrest that the image of the looks as 'mazes' keeps the verse busy with a sense of labyrinthine exploration. 'Entangled' crystallizes and refines the mood of a stanza marked by deftly un-entangled presentation of increasing entanglement. The entangling mazes of Asia's looks reverse the implicit scenario of the lyric: that of an onlooker admiring the transformed Asia. The 'mazes' could, how-ever, also be those engendered by 'the onlooker's own amazement'.[19] The lyric dissolves into one another the implications of these readings of 'mazes': that Asia's 'looks' preserve her otherness, and that Asia's unknowable being can be approached only through (and may be indis-tinguishable from) the speaker's idealizing desires. It is Shelley's achievement to make his lyric's 'one state of feeling' accommodate multiple shadings and nuances without fissuring or fracturing into disparate moods.

Throughout, Shelley's figures Platonize yet undo Platonic distinc-tions. So the 'atmosphere' (l. 58) through which Asia's 'divinity' makes itself felt also 'Shrouds thee wheresoe'er thou shinest' (l. 59); alliteration joins what sense ought to, but, uncannily, does not, put asunder: shining and shrouding. The moment is typical of a lyric that is ecstatic and controlled, pressing towards finality of utterance while allowing for continual modification. Shelley exploits the eager intent-ness offered by a trochaic metre. By contrast, the movement and mood of Byron's 'She Walks in Beauty', composed in iambic tetrameters, are themselves 'mellow'd to that tender light' (l. 5) which the poem praises.[20] Byron, too, is concerned with the indefinable, 'the nameless grace / Which waves in every raven tress' (ll. 8–9); yet where Shelley points up and relishes paradox, Byron smooths potential paradox into extravagant compliment: 'And all that's best of dark and bright / Meet in her aspect and her eyes' (ll. 3–4). Byron's idealizing is evocative –

19 Armstrong, p. 135.
20 Byron's poem is quoted from vol. iii of *Lord Byron: The Complete Poetical Works* (Oxford, 1981), ed. Jerome J. McGann.

the opening four words elegantly resist paraphrase – but the process of idealizing is not simultaneously performed and scrutinized as in Shelley's poem. In Byron's lyric, idealizing has the strengths and limitations of a mode that is, for all its formality, still in touch with the tones of the drawing room. 'She Walks in Beauty' celebrates a 'She' whose potentially symbolic status is only an urbane hint; 'Life of Life' entangles us in a maze where what is 'real' is continually redefined.

Shelley's initial rhyme of 'enkindle' and 'dwindle' is the basis for Daniel Hughes's admirable reading of the lyric as 'a quick *forming* out of motion, an extremely unstable, but still definite point of coherence and completion'.[21] This 'quick *forming* out of motion' is evident in the lyric; throughout, 'motion' is both a threat to and the condition of '*forming*'. 'Dwindle' (l. 50) may intimate extinction; in the same breath, though, it invites us to prize Asia's 'smiles' because of the impermanent radiance which they confer. The extra stress in 'Make the cold air fire' (l. 51) stabilizes our sense of this radiance, a radiance which is, none the less, composed of unstable opposites; the smiles do not so much turn 'cold air' into 'fire' as 'Make' what was, and still is, 'cold air' 'fire'.[22]

As the poem unfolds, the process of '*forming*', of eloquent but provisional realizations, persists. For instance, in the final stanza, 'dim shapes are clad with brightness' (l. 67). This tribute to Asia as 'Lamp of Earth' goes beyond saying that once dim shapes are now bright; it allows for the co-existence of dimness and brightness, for the fact that Asia's brightness is borne witness to by the very dimness of the shapes clad in her sight-defeating brightness. The paradox builds on previous paradoxes. So the second and third stanzas subtilize and qualify the opening stanza's concern with looking. Almost nonchalantly stanza three gives up the attempt to see which stanzas one and two address. In the line 'Fair are others; – none beholds thee' (l. 60), 'beholds' suggests a contemplative calm that goes beyond gazing, a calm which the poem, with excited composure, accepts it cannot attain. So far as any permanent state is reached, it is the state of being 'lost forever' (l. 65) with which the stanza closes; such 'loss' fuses inability to sustain apprehension with, more positively, a loss of self or usual state of consciousness.

21 Daniel Hughes, 'Kindling and Dwindling: The Poetic Process in Shelley', *Keats-Shelley Journal*, xiii (1964), p. 18.
22 See discussion in Armstrong of the way language 'quivers endlessly between negation and assertion' in this line, p. 135.

In stanza two the lyric voice has not yet conceded the inevitable separateness (from the 'thou' it addresses) which is one aspect of the 'loss' described in stanza three, an aspect attested to by the appearance at the end of stanza three of the word 'I'. Stanza two searches for origins as the smiles which 'Make the cold air fire' turn into limbs 'burning / Through the vest which seems to hide them' (ll. 54–5). Bloom speaks of the phrase 'seems to hide' as 'wonderfully ambiguous'; the vest does not hide the limbs 'for they burn through the vest; yet the vest does hide them, because it seems to hide them'.[23] It is an ambiguity, a doubleness of sense, designed to reinforce an impression of indivisibility and singleness. And, straightaway, the paradox of 'limbs' which are and are not at one with the vest they burn through is subjected to a comparison; the limbs burn 'As the radiant lines of morning / Through the clouds ere they divide them' (ll. 56–7). But, as if forestalling the deconstructive reflex which insists that comparisons concede unlikeness in the act of asserting likeness, Shelley's comparison sustains the same dizzying sense of twoness-in-one of the original; in both cases that which 'seems to hide' makes possible what is 'burning' or 'radiant'. So self-aware is the writing that mode mirrors theme; the poem's words seem to hide the very subject which exists by virtue of accomplished admissions of inadequacy, admissions which culminate in the final couplet, 'Till they [the souls of whom thou lovest] fail, as I am failing, / Dizzy, lost . . . yet unbewailing!' (ll. 70–1). Bloom is right to emphasize 'Till', with its implication that 'Fail they must';[24] the glide from walking with lightness (l. 69) to failing accepts without fuss, so far as the visionary project of the lyric (and the lyrical drama) is concerned, the necessary involvement in one another of success and failure. The poem's 'I' refuses to bewail the 'failing' of, among other things, poetic inspiration. Not the least of the flickering oppositions held in temporarily unified suspension by this fine poem is its status both as process and product.

3

Of course 'Life of Life' is part of a larger work; the foregoing discussion seeks less to oppose than to modify Rajan's account of the role performed by lyric in the lyrical drama. My reading privileges the lyric as

---

23 Bloom, p. 127.
24 Bloom, p. 127.

a moment when, without sacrifice of complexity, *Prometheus Unbound* alters the way it signifies, seeming to incarnate its significances within a brief verbal span. More usually, the self is less refined out of existence in Shelley's lyrics than it is in 'Life of Life'. Indeed, Ronald Tetreault argues that, for Shelley, 'The lyric allowed for the exploration and expression of his inner life, but its concerns remained too uniquely private.'[25] Yet Shelley's negotiations with the 'uniquely private' resolve only ambiguously into evocations of 'some one state of feeling'. His early lyrics often safeguard the 'uniquely private' by containing, even burying, suggestions of privacy within an inherited or generalizing lyric idiom. 'Mutability', for instance, builds towards the assertion, 'Man's yesterday may ne'er be like his morrow; / Nought may endure but Mutability' (ll. 15–16). But this epigrammatic condensation of a famous topos comes at the end of a poem whose figurative restlessness – 'We are as clouds' (l. 1), 'Or like forgotten lyres' (l. 5) – implies an impatience with epigram's offer of closure; 'we' bears a strong, if hidden, personal signature in the poem, which seeks controlling definition of experience's refusal to submit to control. This tug shapes the poem's form; the quatrains are tightly rhymed and the iambics mimic a headlong intensity, and yet the feminine rhymes in the first and last stanzas, plus the expertly different pace at which each quatrain moves, enact a chafing against submission to 'one state of feeling'; emotionally and thematically, oppositions meet and indeed collapse in on one another: on the one hand, 'no second motion brings / One mood or modulation like the last' (ll. 7–8); on the other hand, 'It is the same!' (l. 13). The effect is of an undercurrent of private feeling both shaping and ruffling the linguistic surface of the lyric.

'Stanzas. – April, 1814' is another early poem whose plangencies derive from Shelley's oblique dealings with the 'uniquely private'. These dealings are 'oblique' in that Shelley addresses himself as 'thou',[26] instructing himself to cut his emotional losses, 'Tempt not with one last tear thy friend's ungentle mood' (l. 6); and they are 'oblique' because Shelley alternates between suppression and revelation of feeling, intermingling stoicism and 'dereliction' (l. 8), and

---

[25] Tetreault, p. 121.

[26] 'O! there are spirits of the air', which Mary Shelley says was 'addressed in idea to Coleridge' (quoted from *The Poems of Shelley: Volume 1: 1804–1817*, ed. Geoffrey Matthews and Kelvin Everest (London and New York, 1989), p. 448), also addresses a 'thou' in a manner that can be construed as self-address.

making a skilful rhythmic music out of the intermingling, employing description to carry the reader both away from and towards the poem's emotional centre of gravity. Donald Davie argues that 'the "Stanza, written at Bracknell" can control self-pity by controlled and judicious phrasing',[27] and the ability to 'control self-pity' is also evident in 'Stanzas. – April, 1814'.

It is instructive to compare the poem with 'The Serpent Is Shut Out from Paradise', written in Shelley's final year. In an implicitly self-descriptive image, 'Stanzas. – April, 1814' refers to 'dim shades' that 'complicate strange webs of melancholy mirth' (ll. 11, 12), and both this poem and the later lyric deal with, and in, 'complication'. In the first Shelley is returning to his 'sad and silent home' (l. 9) after an emotional entanglement (with Cornelia Boinville Turner) has come to an end; in the second, addressed to Edward and Jane Williams, Shelley alludes to the marital problems that make his a 'cold home' (l. 25). Both poems long for an escape from complication, using similar tropes to convey this longing. In 'Stanzas. – April, 1814' Shelley writes,

> The cloud shadows of midnight possess their own repose,
>   For the weary winds are silent, or the moon is in the deep:
> Some respite to its turbulence unresting ocean knows;
>   Whatever moves, or toils, or grieves, hath its appointed sleep.
>   (ll. 17–20)

The stylized distancing of human emotion in these lines, part and parcel of the poetry's absorption in its own rhythmic virtuosity, is striking. The lines convey what is at once an emotional presence and absence on Shelley's part: they speak eloquently of (by saying nothing about) his own 'turbulence' and exclusion from the universal 'repose' and 'respite' they describe. 'Thou in the grave shalt rest' (l. 21), the beginning of the next stanza, is perfectly judged not to disturb the effect achieved here. It is an effect that contrasts intriguingly with the weighty confessionalism of the line in Wordsworth's 'Ode to Duty' which may have been the younger poet's starting-point, at any rate in lines 17–20: 'I long for a repose that ever is the same'.[28] Shelley's poem

---

27 Donald Davie, *Purity of Diction in English Verse*, enlarged edn (1967; London, 1969), p. 147.
28 'Ode to Duty', l. 40, quoted from William Wordsworth, *Poetical Works*, ed. Thomas Hutchinson, new ed. Ernest de Selincourt (1936; London, Oxford and New York, 1969).

declines to posit so unbearably revealed a centre of self; indeed, we may feel that its deepest longing is to keep the music coming: 'Thy remembrance, and repentance, and deep musings are not free / From the music of two voices and the light of one sweet smile' (ll. 23–4). This is elegantly done, but the pacing is too adroitly managed for the poem's good: 'remembrance' trips rather cheaply into 'repentance', while 'deep' attaches itself unprofoundly to 'musings'. The final intimation that 'one sweet smile' has all along been haunting the poet serves, rather, to underscore the fact that the poem has been more than half in love with its own lyric artifice.

To adapt P. H. Butter's account of 'A Summer-Evening Church-yard', another poem first published in the *Alastor* volume, 'Stanzas. – April, 1814' is a 'product of an immature poet of genius'.[29] 'The Serpent Is Shut Out from Paradise' is the product of a poet whose maturity shows in his readiness to take emotional risks, to trade the merely accomplished for the dramatization of involuntary stops and starts of feeling. So in the sixth stanza, which could be seen as a reworking of lines 17–20 of 'Stanzas. – April, 1814', Shelley reverts to a pattern established in the first stanza. In both the first and the sixth stanzas the first line strives for a mellifluous, apparently single-toned literariness: 'The serpent is shut out from Paradise' (l. 1); 'The crane o'er seas and forests seeks her home' (l. 41). In both stanzas this literariness gives way to something closer to conversational utterance, guarded in the first instance ('I, too, must seldom seek again / Near happy friends a mitigated pain' (ll. 7–8)), almost histrionic in the second ('Doubtless there is a place of peace / Where my weak heart and all its throbs will cease' (ll. 47–8)). Where 'Stanzas. – April, 1814' was artfully oblique, 'The Serpent Is Shut Out from Paradise' intermittently verges on the embarrassingly explicit, as line 48 reveals. The line is as unprotected an expression of self-pity as the most ardent anti-Shelleyan could wish. And yet it is only one phase in a poem whose workings are, tonally and emotionally, far more demanding than those in 'Stanza. – April, 1814'.

The poem cannot, in Mill's phrase, communicate 'some one state of feeling', because it finds out as it unfolds that its feelings are not single. Tension run through the piece. The first line ruffles the 'literariness'

---

[29] Quoted from Percy Bysshe Shelley, *'Alastor' and Other Poems; 'Prometheus Unbound' with Other Poems; 'Adonais'*, ed. P. H. Butter (London and Glasgow, 1970), p. 249.

mentioned above by coupling Biblical allusion with wryly private joking (Shelley was nicknamed 'the snake');[30] lament for the serpent's exclusion blends with recognition of the fact that other people's paradises are better off without serpents. The poem is at emotional cross-purposes with itself throughout; Shelley feels he should deny himself the 'mitigated pain' which the company of his friends offers, only to argue that being the object of their 'Pity' (l. 12) is unbearable. In stanza three the poem articulates the impasse which the workings of the first two stanzas have intimated: 'The very comfort which they [the looks of his friends] minister / I scarce can bear; yet I, / (So deeply is the arrow gone) / Should quickly perish if it were withdrawn' (ll. 21–4). 'I scarce can bear'; 'Should quickly perish': these seem the stock terms on which Romantic emotionalism might depend. Yet these intensities coexist with the poised movement of the lines across the modified ottava rima[31] as well as with fidelity to the rhythms of speech (in, say, the recoil of 'yet I', or the painful semi-jest of the parenthesis which follows). The result is not to damp down the 'sense of unrelieved, even unrelievable, frustration'[32] which William Keach detects in the poem, but to add to it the further sense that the poet is driven, and knows he is being driven, to play a 'forced part' (l. 28) in his own poem.

This is not to accuse Shelley of insincerity; it is, rather, to observe the way the poem authenticates his unhappiness at having to assume 'the idle mask / Of author' (ll. 29–30); to observe, too, the way the poem seems to open up fractional silences after its assertions and qualifications, silences in which the provisionality of what has just been said is at once muted and acknowledged. Certainly it is to the poem's credit that Shelley does not wholly persuade us he has 'relieved / His heart with words' (ll. 51–2). The lyric allows overstatement to co-exist with indeterminacy, false notes to play against candour, explicit revelation to pass into reticence and doubt, the 'bundle of accident and incoherence that sits down to breakfast', in Yeats's words,[33] to enter into dialogue with the self projected by lyric. 'These verses were too sad / To send to you' (ll. 54–5) steps out of the frame of

[30] See PP, p. 447.
[31] See William Keach, Shelley's Style (New York and London, 1984), hereafter Keach, for the form as a possible reflection of 'Byron's influence on the poem', p. 218.
[32] Keach, p. 219.
[33] W. B. Yeats, 'A General Introduction for my Work' (1937), quoted from W.

the lyric; there is both art in and an undefended rawness about this disclaimer that contrasts with the effect of the graceful apology at the end of 'Stanzas written in Dejection – December 1818, Near Naples', where Shelley regrets his poem's 'untimely moan' (l. 40). In 'Stanzas written in Dejection' Shelley's surprises – the self-effacing attention to nature, the delayed entrance of the self-pitying self, the self-consciousness about self-pity – are woven harmoniously into the poem's texture; they do not enforce recognition of a gulf or link between the suffering man and the creating mind. In 'The Serpent Is Shut Out from Paradise' Shelley shapes an impressively self-divided lyricism out of his sense of the difficulties posed by the 'uniquely private'; the poem allows us to eavesdrop on the interplay between what Nietzsche calls 'the lyric genius and the allied non-genius'.[34]

4

'The Serpent Is Shut Out from Paradise' makes a last-minute appeal to its audience (Edward and Jane Williams) by praising them for their capacity to 'feel another's woe' (l. 56); in doing so, it not only moves out of its lyric space into lives beyond itself, it also draws those lives back into the lyric space it seems to be abandoning. Other late lyrics both undermine and protect their autonomy. 'When the lamp is shattered'[35] wins a bleak lyric triumph out of themes of failure and aftermath, loss and survival. If ever a poem seemed intent on evoking 'some one state of feeling', this is it; but the poem proves to be more intricate. Indeed, if it does impress as conveying 'one state of feeling' it does so because of a driving intensity that extends, even as it elaborates, the poem's initial position. Loss refuses to be as absolute as the series of figures in the opening stanza intimates, and passes into survival. 'When the lips have spoken / Loved accents are soon forgot' (ll. 7–8) may dispose of 'Loved accents', yet the next stanza asserts the persistence of songs that are not songs but 'sad dirges' (l. 13) which come into being when 'the spirit is mute' (l. 12). Survival, living on

B. Yeats, *Selected Criticism and Prose*, ed. with intro. and notes by A. Norman Jeffares (London, 1980), p. 255.

[34] *The Birth of Tragedy*, section 5; quoted from Friedrich Nietzsche, *'The Birth of Tragedy' and 'The Case of Wagner'*, trans. with commentary by Walter Kaufmann (New York, 1967), p. 50.

[35] Quoted from text in Chernaik, pp. 254–6.

after loss or hurt, turns out to be the poem's true theme; 'music and splendour' may 'Survive not the lamp and the lute' (ll. 9–10), but something does survive, something that denies the reader the easy frisson of complete loss the poem seems to offer.

With this and the emotional plot which unfolds in the third stanza in mind, the reader may find the clarity of lines 7–8 more apparent than real: 'Loved accents are soon forgot' but how soon is 'soon'? The line wants to make comparable the forgetting of loved accents and the other losses described in the stanza; yet in the very attempt to make the emotional conform to laws governing the physical Shelley alerts us to subjective pressures, smuggling back the lyric subject seemingly suppressed by the poem. Again, in the second stanza, the poem's unique timbre appears, briefly and self-reflexively, to be suggested, a sad dirge written out of the spirit's muteness. Throughout, there is a contest between images that seek some conclusive definition of failure and the awareness that emotional closure is hard to come by. Failure has many gradations as the final stanza indicates through its use of a future tense and phrases that chart successive stages in some imagined divestiture of dignity; when the last line arrives, in all its spondaic finality ('When leaves fall and cold winds come'), there is less a sense of reaching a conclusion than of realizing more fully what is involved by the word 'endure' in the earlier lines, 'The weak one is singled / To endure what it once possest' (ll. 19–20). By echoing the 'when' construction which governs earlier lines, but this time leads nowhere beyond itself, the last line rounds off yet questions previous attempts to argue through images, holding the poem open to the unarguable rigours suggested by falling leaves and cold winds.

The tussle between sobered delight in the 'magic circle' ('To Jane. The Recollection', l. 44) drawn by lyric art and awareness of realities outside art's magic circle vitalizes the late poems to Jane Williams. Often it is hard to know who has the upper hand: the idealizing lyricist or the sceptic leaning over his shoulder. In the last stanza of 'To Jane: "The keen stars were twinkling" ', as Keach points out, 'The world of ideal lyric unity is explicitly recognized as being "far from ours" '.[36] Yet the poem wins through (originally Shelley concluded the poem with 'won' rather than 'one')[37] to its glimpse of 'ideal lyric unity' more

---

[36] Keach, p. 228.
[37] See Chernaik, p. 261; Keach also comments on this detail, emphasizing what it reveals about 'a performance or exertion of the interpretive will', p. 228.

buoyantly than Keach allows. The ingenious use to which Shelley puts his arrangement of line-length and rhyme, so that every sixth line has a clinching effect, contributes to this buoyancy. From the start, the poem privileges the 'voice' of its addressee, who serves as source and correlative of poetic inspiration, a muse figure the more credible for the uninflated nature of the poet's address: 'the notes were not sweet 'till you sung them / Again' (ll. 5–6). Here Jane creates and discovers harmony in the same breath; later, the voice's power to confer value is stressed as it spiritualizes 'the strings without soul' (l. 11). Even here there is, because of the comparison launched in line seven ('moon's soft splendour' (l. 7) is to 'faint cold starlight' (l. 8) as 'voice most tender' (l. 10) is to 'strings without soul'), a suggestion that Jane's power derives from some lucky accord between the natural and the human. But in the second stanza this not wholly logical suggestion drops away: whether 'the moon sleep a full hour later' (l. 14) the impact of Jane's singing is not diminished; at the end of the poem it is the creative effect of her 'voice' (l. 20) which is praised. If this leaves the poem open to the charge that what it exhibits is merely the 'exertion of the interpretive will', in Keach's phrase, it should be noted that Shelley seeks to silence the charge by speaking of the voice as '*revealing* / A tone / Of some world far from ours' (ll. 20–2; my emphasis), a classic instance of deconstructive critical strategies being outwitted in advance by a poem. Shelley protects his poem against its and our scepticism by implying that it illustrates through its workings the autonomy of song which is its theme, and that it reveals – not just fabricates – a reality 'far from ours'.

That my commentary on 'To Jane: "The keen stars were twinkling" ' ends with the phrase whose challenge to 'lyric unity' I claim the poem is able to absorb is significant; it reveals how precarious any defence of these poems against their deconstructive impulses is likely to be. None the less, Shelley's formal choices in this poem and the companion pieces, 'To Jane. The Invitation' and 'To Jane. The Recollection', are designed to play down, though not to silence, their less assimilable moods. The flowing couplets of 'To Jane. The Invitation', for instance, protect the poet's discovery of 'one moment's good' (l. 44) by suspending it in a contiguous flow of thoughts and feelings. The poem looks before and after, glancing at the humdrum misery of 'the unpaid bill' (l. 35), accepting the likely return of 'Reflexion' (l. 33) and 'Sorrow' (l. 34), and tacitly allowing that there will be times when, unlike the present, the 'soul' will need to 'repress / Its music lest it should not find / An echo in another's mind' (ll. 24–6), lines where

the 'echo' enacted by rhyme holds at arm's length the fear of echoless-
ness. Yet the poem takes on board and manages to accommodate these
obstacles to lyric celebration of the 'Radiant Sister of the day' (l. 47).
What is imaginatively projected in the final paragraph is a folding of
the 'multitudinous' (l. 65) into 'one' (l. 68):

> And the multitudinous
> Billows murmur at our feet
> Where the earth and ocean meet,
> And all things seem only one
> In the universal Sun. –   (ll. 65–9)

Although the metre is trochaic, 'seem' attracts a good deal of attention
here. And yet for all its momentariness, possible illusoriness and
potential vulnerability to strains both within and without ('To Jane.
The Recollection' will bring such strains to the fore), the vision
attained at the end of 'To Jane. The Invitation' is richly, if complexly,
affirmative. There is an often justifiable wariness of the unitary in
contemporary criticism of Romantic poets. Despite (or because of)
this, it is worth re-emphasizing that, without the impulse to imagine
states in which 'all things seem only one', the contrary impulses
chartable in many of Shelley's finest poems would lose much of their
power.

Notes on Contributors

Bernard Beatty is a Senior Lecturer in English at the University of Liverpool. He is academic editor of the *Byron Journal*, and has published *Byron's Don Juan and Other Poems* (1987), and co-edited *Byron and the Limits of Fiction* (1988). He has also published numerous articles on Romanticism, Bunyan, Dryden, Rochester, and others.

Richard Cronin teaches at the University of Glasgow. He is the author of *Shelley: Poetic Thoughts, Colour and Experience in 19th Century Verse*, and *Imagining India*.

Kelvin Everest is A. C. Bradley Professor of Modern Literature at the University of Liverpool. He has written *Coleridge's Secret Ministry* and *English Romantic Poetry*, edited and contributed to several volumes of essays on Romantic Literature, and is currently editing Shelley's poems in the Longman 'Annoted English Poets' series.

Edward Larrissy is lecturer in English at the University of Warwick, where he has been Programme Director of the Centre for Research in Philosophy and Literature. He is the author of *William Blake* (1985) in the Rereading Literature series; of *Reading Twentieth Century Poetry: The Language of Gender and Objects* (1990); and of the forthcoming *Yeats the Poet: The Measures of Difference*.

Vincent Newey is Professor of English at the University of Leicester. He is the author of *Cowper's Poetry: A Critical Study and Reassessment* (1982) and joint editor of *Byron and the Limits of Fiction* (1988) and *Literature and Nationalism* (1991). His other publications include a range of Articles on Puritan writers, Victorian fiction and, especially, the Romantic poets. He is currently working on the theme of Romantic subjectivity and 'self-creation'. He was a founding editor of the *Bulletin of the British Association for Romantic Studies* and is currently one of the editors of the *Byron Journal*.

Michael O'Neill is a Senior Lecturer in English at the University of Durham. He is the author of *The Human Mind's Imaginings: Conflict and Achievement in Shelley's Poetry* (Oxford, 1989), *Percy Bysshe Shelley: A Literary Life* (London, 1989), and (with Gareth Reeves) *Auden, MacNeice, Spender: The Thirties Poetry* (London, 1992); he is also the author of *The Stripped Bed* (London, 1990), a book of poems, and a co-editor of *Poetry Durham*.

Timothy Webb is Professor of English at the University of Bristol, having previously held appointments at Leeds and York. His publications include *The Violet in the Crucible: Shelley and Translation* (1976), *Shelley: A Voice not Understood* (1977), *English Romantic Hellenism 1700–1824* (1982), and annotated selections from Shelley (1977) and Yeats (1991). He is General Editor of the Penguin Yeats and has been editor of the *Keats-Shelley Review* (originally Memorial Bulletin) since 1977.

DATE DUE